Embodied Prayer

Embodied Prayer

Harmonizing Body *and* Soul

Celeste Snowber Schroeder

TRIUMPH™ BOOKS
Liguori, Missouri

Published by Triumph™ Books
Liguori, Missouri
An Imprint of Liguori Publications

All quotes from the Bible are taken from the New Revised Standard Version
(NRSV) unless otherwise noted.

Small sections from Chapters 6, 11, and 12 have been adapted from my
articles which have been previously published as: "Lament and Light," *Modern Liturgy*, Vol. 20, No. 7 (September 1993), "Dance as a Posture of Joy"
Crux, Vol. XXX, No. 1 (March 1994), and "The Washing of Feet: A Bodily
Prayer," *Sacred Dance Guild Journal*, Vol. 36, No. 2 (Winter 1993).

Any names used as anecdotes within this book have been changed in order
not to identify the individuals. The examples do not necessarily reflect one
person's experience, but have been composites of various situations.

Library of Congress Cataloging-in-Publication Data

Schroeder, Celeste Snowber.
    Embodied prayer : harmonizing body and soul / Celeste Snowber
Schroeder. — 1st ed.
        p.   cm.
    Includes bibliographical references and index.
    ISBN 0-89243-782-0
    1. Prayer—Christianity.   2. Gesture in worship.   3. Religious
dance, Modern.   4. Body, Human—Religious aspects—Christianity.
I. Title.
BV215.S36   1994
248.3'2—dc20
                                                       94-34024
                                                          CIP

For Tom

CONTENTS

Acknowledgments

Just as there are many parts of the body, and all are needed, there are many parts of writing a book. I could not possibly list all the people and experiences that have shaped and inspired me along the way in the formation of this book. I am particularly grateful for those people who have encouraged me as I have pioneered in the field of dance and Christian spirituality over the years. Many participants in my workshops, and students in my college classes, have given me the privilege to dance into their own journeys. Through their openness to exploring the body in the spiritual life, I have been able to see lives broken open in fullness. I have learned as much from them as they have learned from me.

I want to particularly thank those who have truly served as "midwives" to me in the task of writing this book. Many have encouraged and supported me and read this manuscript in the several drafts it has gone through. Fay Lapka and Eugene Peterson initially gave me helpful suggestions. Susan McCaslin, Marcia Fretheim, and Kaija Pepper all gave keen editorial remarks, and I'm grateful for their "third eyes" as well as their ongoing encouragement and friendship. I have been privileged to have others as well who have walked alongside me and believed in my work: Laurie Peterson, Connie Moker-Wernikowski, Boelle Kirby, Toni and Mardi Dolfo-Smith, Kerry McFarlane Bell, Judi Reimer, Barbara Pell, and Erica Grimm-Vance.

Fran Robinson continues to let my wings fly as she embodies God's love to me.

My neighbor Nancy Webber graciously let me use her house to write much of this manuscript, so I could have a quiet place to work. Without this space, I would surely be still writing in the midst of my own busy home.

Tim, Marcia, Sara, and Erin Fretheim have been a family to us, and have been a wonderful support.

My mother and father, Frank and Grace Snowber, who have passed away, gave me the freedom long ago to see my body as good and wholesome, to celebrate life with, pray with, and express my innermost parts. My children, Lucas, Caleb, and Micah Schroeder, continue to bring forth the "dancer" inside me, as they bring their energetic bodies to every aspect of life.

Most of all, I thank my husband, Tom, for his ongoing support to me in all my creative endeavors. He has faithfully encouraged me through many pioneering years, in my dances of lament and my dances of joy. He has endured with me in the writing of this book, read and interacted with my chapters, and arranged his work schedule to take care of our children, freeing me to write.

And I thank those whom I have not mentioned.

I thank Patricia Kossmann, my editor at Triumph, for her interest in this manuscript. I am also thankful to Joan Marlow Golan at Triumph for her editorial input. Their enthusiasm has been a great gift to me.

INTRODUCTION

❦

This book is an invitation to experience prayer from the inside out, awakening our souls to God through our bodies. This is not just for those who have some natural sense of movement or for those who are in prime physical shape. It is for all who want to expand the language of prayer with their Maker — and "pray with the bones."

The life of prayer has many contours: asking and listening, reciting and contemplating, speaking and moving. Through each contour we are drawn into communion with our Maker. In this journey of prayer God has given us a remarkable gift that is seldom recognized: our bodies! Many of us have learned either to ignore our bodies or to see them as something to be controlled. This is a far cry from a biblical spirituality that calls us to wholeness — the union of body and spirit with God. There seems to be an unspoken premise in Western culture, that body and soul are divided and disconnected. We listen or pray with our hearts and minds but ignore much of our bodies; we become "disembodied."

1

We are, however, created in God's image — mind,
body, spirit. We are unified whether we like it or not.
I hope to reclaim what has in the past been somewhat forgotten in the Judeo-Christian tradition, a rich
heritage of faith that was expressed not only through
the mind but through heart, bones, arms, fingers, and
postures. The inward grace of God was made visible
through the physicality of the body, from the sways of
lament to the open palms of supplication and the ju-
bilant leaps of celebration. The life of faith was written
on the body, a place of extreme vulnerability. We have
long concentrated on the negative aspects of the body
in this world; it is time for God's people to see the gift
of the body and how the language of the body — or the
language of movement — can be a sacred place of dialogue with our Creator. The body can become a place
where we can listen to our own voice, the voice that
is sometimes muffled by the constant demands of our
lives.

Our bodies will often tell us when it is time to go apart
in solitude, or to recapture the presence of God, if we
can learn to listen. Taut necks, tired backs, or stiff torsos can be a reminder to us that we are pushing too
hard, that our bodies are yearning for balance or attention to the spiritual hunger within. Our lives often allow
room for attention to mental prayer or physical exercise
alone; seldom do we think we can do both at the same
time! Yet even in our verbal prayers, we pray with our
bodies: Breath, voice, and posture are all bodily forms
of expression. As so well put by Catherine de Hueck
Doherty:

Prayer is that hunger for union which never lets go
of us. It beats into our blood with the very beat
of our hearts. It is a thirst that can be quenched
by nothing except God. It's as if one's whole body
is poised on tip-toe, our hands stretching upward
as if to touch the cosmos. The act of praying, like
the act of love, involves movement and effort. You
don't pray like a robot any more than you make love
like one! Prayer is movement, stretching, seeking
holding, finding.... [1]

This book is an invitation to let the act of prayer swell
through our entire bodies, enlarging the capacity of our
bodies to become a sacred space for prayer. This can be a
space where we can express the deepest yearnings of our
hearts, where the prayers of the psalms can be written
on our bodies. We can cultivate prayer, not only in our
hearts and minds, but in our torsos, arms, hands, fingers,
and feet.

Embodied Prayer is intended to complement your own
spiritual journey. It will not give you specific steps and
actions to use as would a manual of classical ballet or aerobics, but it will hopefully unloose the power and beauty
of your own unique movement to incorporate into your
spiritual life. Everyone has the capacity to move, although we will not all become great dancers. It is also
my belief that we all are creative, since we are made in
God's image.

In my work as a liturgical dance artist and educator I have seen many people of all shapes and sizes,
of different ages and from different cultures, in vari-

ous professions and denominations, who have gone from feeling quite uncomfortable with their bodies to being profoundly touched by their experience of welcoming their bodies in prayer. It is not uncommon for men and women to weep as they discover the joy of using their bodies in expressing the very thing that is most important to them: their faith. So I invite you to make friends with your body, too, if you have not already done so, and ultimately to enrich your life of prayer.

This book is divided into three sections. The first section will seek to give a foundation for an embodied faith. It looks at the source of our makeup as whole human beings — God's design for us to be interconnected, woven together in heart and body. A biblical theology of embodied prayer begins with the principle of creation, moving through incarnation and redemption. Creation sets the framework for bodily movement, designed by God from the very beginning. The incarnation of Jesus Christ, the Word becoming flesh, also has great significance for embracing a bodily spirituality. The importance of God's intention for redemption of the whole person, body and soul, is outlined, and its implication for a theology of embodied faith is explored.

Part II moves us through the historical presence of bodily prayer in the Old and New Testament, particularly the psalms, and in Church history. There is a wide spectrum of physical language within the Scriptures relating to supplication, adoration, thanksgiving, praise, and lament. The Psalter has been the Church's map to song and prayer for centuries, a place where prayer becomes an active conversation with God. Filled with the power of visual metaphor, the psalms are a rich source for beginning the journey in bodily prayer. God's people have a legacy of incorporating physical language in prayer — we as a contemporary people of faith can gain inspiration from seeing their spirituality of body and soul. Jesus continues this tradition in his use of postures and prayer, but also by giving us an example of a bodily way of being in the world. His ministry is characterized by heart being met through body: touching the sick, washing the disciples' feet, breaking bread, embracing the children. The Church has in its history an extremely rich heritage in utilizing ritualized movement, dance, drama, and the body, and I have included an overview of some of the ways movement has been used to encourage us in our journey today.

Part III is a pragmatic invitation to encounter God through embodied prayer. Listening to God, healing, lament, and celebration are looked at in depth. You will be invited to go beyond purely mechanical prayer to "the prayer of the heart": to see embodied prayer as a complement to the contemplative life. These chapters will also give you some of the inspiration not only to encounter bodily prayer, but to live as embodied people — to live in fullness of body, mind, and spirit, and ultimately to listen to the fire of God in the places of your hearts and bodies.

At the end of the book there are practical exercises/improvisations in embodied prayer that you can enter. I would invite you to incorporate these in your daily prayer life. It will be important to find a space that can be relatively private and set apart to explore this dimension of your spirituality. Some exercises will be for personal use, and others can be utilized in group settings or retreats. They are meant only as guides, not exact recipes, so you can modify them to your own faith journey.

It is my hope that this book will allow you to discover the gift of your body, not only in the life of faith, but also in understanding what it means to be fully human. For those of you who have already included your bodies in the spiritual journey, my hope is that you will be given food for your ongoing journey in embodied prayer. May we all be nourished by praying with our bones!

Note

1. Catherine de Hueck Doherty, *Soul of My Soul: Reflections from a Life of Prayer* (Notre Dame, Ind.: Ave Maria Press, 1985).

Part One

GENESIS OF
EMBODIED PRAYER

Chapter 1

MOVEMENT

The Inner and Outer Language

The Dance of Life in the Womb

My extended belly pulsed the life within me. Even an outside observer glancing on could see my belly moving into various contorted shapes. Movement of tiny feet, arms, legs, heads, was a constant reminder of the miracle of creation forming within my womb. Life burst, even in my stillness! Breathing, living, and pulsing within the secure place of my womb, our two babies were being formed in what I call the womb-studio: the studio of God. A sign of the Maker's birthing within a woman, the language of movement is present in the beginnings of life.

So beautifully portrayed in the Gospel of Luke[1] is the account of Elizabeth's baby at the greeting of Mary: "The baby leaped in her womb, and Elizabeth was filled with the Holy Spirit." Leaping and kicking are this baby's vowels; he responds immediately with the fullness of his little body in a dance to the coming Messiah. How appropriate at the beginning of John the Baptist's life that he would respond to God through his body, for John the Baptist was the one who would be remembered for inaugurating the baptism of the body — the cleansing of body and soul. The rite of baptism itself is a reminder that body and soul are connected.

We were designed and created to move from our formation in the womb. Ted Shawn, a well-known pioneer in modern dance, captures this in stating:

> We know that body movement is life itself — our movement begins in the womb before birth and the new-born infant's need for movement is imperative and continuous. When we sleep there is constant movement, our hearts beat, our intestines work; in fact as long as there is life there is movement, and to move is hence to satisfy a basic and eternal need.[2]

From the moment of conception, to living in the womb, to being pushed through the birth canal, a baby does not stop moving. The milestones in an infant's world are passages of movement: rolling, bouncing, sitting, standing, falling, crawling, and eventually graduating to the walking, skipping, jumping, and running of toddlerhood. Each stage of life is filled with holy wonder — the wonder of discovering new ways to move. If we could only remember the delight we had the first time we walked, climbed, skipped, or ran into mother's or father's arms!

The Dance of the Child

Children skip, run, and hop to a dance of their own. Nowhere do we see this with more clarity than in visiting a playground. Brightly colored jackets, messed-up hair, and old sneakers move with vitality as children abandon themselves to the world of play. They engage physically in their world, exhibiting a wide range of movement. Arms reach, knees bend, legs climb, torsos slide, and bodies swing with sheer joy as they play. As adults we are often onlookers to this playful movement, sitting on the sidelines and possibly reminiscing about the time we, too, moved our bodies with little inhibition. We are now too concerned with what our bodies look like: if we are too big, too little, or too awkward, or if we would look too foolish. Do we adhere to the unspoken rule that only the children can play?

Some of us would have to admit that we move vicariously through children as we observe them move and dance with freedom and ease. Children are not as aware of how they look when they move and revel in being kinesthetically alive. They thrive in the world of play, dancing to the rhythm of their own voice. Dancing with ease and spontaneity is so natural for children that Jesus cites children's inclination to dance when describing his generation (Mt 11:16–19, Lk 7:31–35).

To what can I compare this generation? They are like children sitting in the marketplaces and calling out to others: "We played the flute for you, and you did not dance; we sang a dirge, and you did not mourn."

How many times do we wish we could just stretch our torsos up with pure abandon and run or twirl through open fields and sandy beaches as children can? Somehow we have lost something along the way.

The Body As Signature

Children have a "body signature" all their own. Not being overly conscious of what are culturally acceptable ways to move, they are more inclined to respond authentically. Children readily show their feelings and thoughts through physical expression, jumping up and down when excited, hunching over their bodies when upset, or enthusiastically running into a parent's arms for a hug. Unfortunately children eventually learn to be conscious of their bodies — how thin, big, small, or tall they should be — through the persistent images in television, magazines, and billboard advertisements. We are assaulted daily with images of the "ideal beauty." Experts find that the age of children with eating disorders is decreasing. The connection is made at an early age between success and certain body types, although few attain the ideal. The obsession with physical appearance can affect a child's enjoyment of moving and dancing.

Children and adolescents also learn the particular cultural norms about when it is appropriate and not appropriate to move their bodies. In North American culture the football stadium has become a sanctioned place for boys and men to move; there they can jump up and down and swing their arms with exuberance. You may even find some in the sidelines dancing. Why is this same physical response not considered as appropriate for other times of celebration in our culture, such as graduations, weddings, baptisms, or reunions?

Adults have other ways of revealing their unique body signature. The way they hold their heads and torsos, speak with their hands, slouch their backs, walk through an office, or even give a handshake communicates something of who they are. It has been said that it is easier to lie with the lips than the body, and I think this still holds true. Doris Humphrey, a pioneer in modern dance, articulates this as she says:

> Nothing so clearly and inevitably reveals the inner man [woman] more than movement and gesture. It is quite possible, if one chooses, to conceal and dissimulate behind words or paintings or statues or other forms of human expression, but the moment you move you stand revealed, for good or ill, for what you are.[3]

The language of our gestures, postures, and facial expressions often reveals more than all of our eloquent words. Communication experts say that 80–90 percent of our communication is through "body language." It doesn't take an expert to acknowledge that a friend is really having a hard time by reading his/her body language. We have forgotten that movement was once a very expressive language for many of us, particularly when we were children. We can still recover the body as a place for our inner life to move and breathe in a language with little pretense.

We need to learn to listen to the signature of our bodies. In a world that thrives on fast-paced living, consumerism, and production more than being, we often have little time to listen to what our bodies tell us. We think we can train and conquer them as if we were captains in command, not respecting the reality that our bodies may not appreciate being pushed, shoved, and forced through life. Our bodies will often raise their voices to us through other signs: tiredness, tension, stiff necks, aching backs, tense muscles, chronic flus, or general lack of well-being. This does not mean that every ailment has an emotional correlation, but there is an innate connectedness between mind and body that calls out for our attention. Even a cursory glance at the best-sellers in the health section of your local bookstore will substantiate the focus of many researchers and popular authors on the relationship between mind and body.

The body has the capacity to proclaim loudly what is going on within us. We need to *listen,* not only to its bold proclamations but also to its subtle notes of distress. It has been said that our bodies are not *minor* but *major* prophets.[4] Because of our unique makeup, each person will have specific ways his/her own body will teach him/her. I can often tell my life is out of balance when I find myself catching one cold or flu after the other. Never seeming to recuperate, lacking energy, I find the diagnosis is always a virus. I have begun to learn that this is a signal for me to get the Martha and Mary in balance: to make more time for solitude and sabbath. Some people who exhibit persistent problems in their neck or back may need to take time for physical activity — walking, swimming, or other exercise. For others it may take even more serious circumstances, like heart attacks, insomnia, or emotional discord, to get them to listen to their bodies. Whatever the manifestation, it is essential to reclaim our bodies, respecting them and learning to listen to their pulse.

Recovering Our Bodies

The question may be asked, Doesn't Western culture already put enough emphasis on the body? Yes, it does, but sadly it is the wrong emphasis. The focus is on outer appearance, denying the relationship between the body and heart, mind and soul.

Our bodies are like breath — so much a part of us we don't recognize them unless they are out of breath and accelerated or slowed down. Our bodies need the room to feel accepted for how they are, whatever shape, size, or limitations they have. Many times we find ourselves in a space of being in-between; we are not exactly the right weight, shape, or as physically fit as we would hope to be. I would suggest that this place of being in-between is where we may find ourselves most of our life. We live in the in-between more than in our hopes and ideals for who we want to be.

Part of recovering our bodies is accepting our in-between states, our imperfections, and acknowledging that we are clay. Many of us have become estranged from our bodies; it is time to make them friends. They are part of us, and we must invite them back. If we don't, we will become increasingly alienated from ourselves. Recently I was giving a workshop to a group of women in the area of movement and spirituality. In the beginning of the workshop I led them in a basic warm-up, and then we did some simple circle dances. While dancing in a circle, we accompanied ourselves by singing a familiar chorus. This is always a nonthreatening time where the group casually experiences the joy of moving their bodies to the rhythm of the body's own voice. As the workshop progressed, there was opportunity to incorporate the body in deeper dialogue with God. After the workshop was over, a woman relayed to me her experience over the last several years of physically not being able to sing. Singing was her love; because of particular circumstances this had become virtually impossible for her, and she grieved over it immensely. As she participated in inviting her body to move, her voice was released from deep within her being. It was almost as if when she invited the other parts of her body to sing, not only could her lungs finally be filled with air, but her vocal chords were released. Her joy was profound, for she could welcome back something very precious in her life that had been lost. As I witnessed this remarkable transformation, I could enter her joy and learn again the timeless truth that our bodies are interconnected: voice, limbs, emotions, mind, and gestures. Her body brought the music back from the depths where it had been lost.

Music also has the capacity to bring our bodies back. Many years ago while my husband and I were living in Saskatchewan, the heart of the Canadian prairies, each week we had the opportunity to take several people from our church to the local nursing home. My husband was serving as a pastor of a small rural church, and along with some of the senior members of the congregation, we were asked to work with some of the most unfortunate people, including those who had little contact with loved ones. Our approach was to invite them to sing using simple gestures to accompany the hymns. They were sitting in wheelchairs and beds most of the time, and we wanted to provide an opportunity for them to use other parts of their bodies, even if minimally, giving arms, fingers, hands, mouths, and facial expressions a chance to come alive. We would actually move the residents' hands, bringing them together to clap or just swinging them to the gentle rhythm of a hymn. One incident remains etched in my memory — it is of a woman I will call Edna, slumped over in her wheelchair, able to use only minimal movement, her face dropped down to her left shoulder, worn out from poor physical health; her body was tired. Edna had not spoken to anyone in over two years; not a word had issued from her well-worn lips. No one, including family, nursing-home staff, and friends, could get her to speak. One day we were singing an old hymn, "I come to the garden alone while the dew is still on the roses....." As we were singing this hymn, her mouth started moving, and something deep within her moved her to speak. This old, familiar hymn unlocked the speech tied up in her body. She proclaimed, "Oh, oh, that was lovely!" The director of the nursing home said that after this experience she began slowly to speak again; her family were stunned and grateful. I have often thought of Edna, who really taught me about the power of gesture and music to unlock our deepest emotions and memories. We are connected, no matter what, and even in the twilight of life the body has a way of guiding us back to our heart.

I relate these incidents because they are examples of very ordinary people recovering their bodies. They were not engaged in extreme physical activity, nor had they read contemporary manuals on the body and soul, or even been in an established exercise program. They did have the opportunity to use a part of their bodies that had lain dormant for too long. Recovering our bodies does not necessarily mean taking monumental strides. Sometimes it can be as simple as being attentive to our breath, stretching an open palm to God, or expressing a dance of frustration in the private space of our bedroom.

Seeing our physicality as a gift — this is the most important element in recovering our bodies. Sometimes the eyes of our heart must be changed to see this, but it takes the eyes of our body to make it so. God's gift to us is part of our intrinsic makeup. For too long we have been estranged from our bodies; now is the time to bring them back so we may become whole people, the whole people whom God made us to be.

This chapter began with movement from the womb and ended with an elderly person in the final stage of mortality. God has etched us with gestures in our bodies as part of the wonderful fabric of who we are. As

Ruth St. Denis, a famous modern dancer, said in such simple terms:

> Pure dance has no bounds. The infant begins to dance at its mother's knee. Old age should have its gestures to express love and serenity no less.[5]

We may not be trained dancers, eloquent in movement, or have ideal body types, but there is a dance within us waiting to be ignited and birthed. Moving is integral to being human. May we again find the joy we did as children and welcome our bodies in our spiritual journeys.

Notes

1. See Luke 1:39–45.

2. Ted Shawn, *Dance We Must* (New York: Haskell House, 1971), p. 13.

3. Doris Humphrey, in Walter Sorell, ed., *The Dance Has Many Faces* (New York: Columbia University Press, 1966), p. 113.

4. Flora Slosson Wuellner, *Prayer and Our Bodies* (Nashville, Tenn.: Upper Room, 1987), p. 32.

5. Ruth St. Denis, taken from *Denishawn Magazine* (1924–25) as quoted in Jean Morrison Brown, ed., *The Vision of Modern Dance* (Princeton, N.J.: Princeton Book Co., 1979), p. 24.

Chapter 2

AND GOD BREATHED

Spirit and Body

ℂ—————— Ꭳ ——————

In the beginning God created the heavens and the
earth...the sky and the waters...the creatures of
all kinds...and God created humankind...in the
image of God they were created; male and female
God created them.

God is the author and creator of our bodies. This well-
known passage in the first chapter of the Creation story
in Genesis powerfully tells about the creating of man and
woman — in the Maker's own image. The image that
man and woman were given was not one of amorphous
vapor, but that of living persons, clothed in all the intri-
cacies of the body: organs, blood, muscles, flesh, bones,
and with the language of the body.

God breathed into man and woman the breath of life;
bones and flesh became enlivened with spirit. The Creation story tells us that God made us from the dust of
the ground, the humus of the earth, and breathed life

into our very bones (Gen 2:7). The Hebrew literally tells
us that "God breathed in the nostrils the breath of life
and the human became a *nephesh*," most often translated
as *soul*. The passage does not say that the human was sup-
plied with a soul as some other attachment to the body,
but by the breath of God the human became a living
body-soul, a living human being. So man and woman in
their total essence are souls. As articulated by Old Testament scholar Johannes Pedersen, "Soul and body are so
intimately united that a distinction cannot be made between them. They are more than 'united': the body is the
soul in its outward form."[1] In the beginning of creation
we were designed as one: body-soul.

Breath is a physical reminder to us that it is God
who breathed life into us; we were literally "inspired"
into being, breathed into being by God. The Hebrew
understanding of the breath is closely associated with the
soul and the desire of human beings. The psalmist proclaims, "Let everything that breathes praise the Lord!"
(Ps 150:6) The author of Proverbs says, "The human
spirit is the lamp of the Lord, searching every innermost
part" (Prov 20:27, RSV). The Hebrew word translated in
this passage for human spirit is the word *neshama,* one
of the Hebrew words used for breath. The verse could
just as well be translated as "The breath of man and
woman is the lamp of the Lord." Our breath is a gift
and has become such a natural part of us that we forget
we are actually breathing, but without it we cannot live.
The Spirit of God keeps on breathing into us, forming,
shaping, and transforming us on our journeys of faith.
Our bodily prayer can be breath in and of itself, breath-

ing out our desires, pain, hurts, joys, visions, hopes, and longings.

Breath is one of the first bodily functions we come in contact with in bodily prayer. As we move our body, we become in touch with our pulse, and the rhythm and presence of our breath. Nancy Roth has said, "Prayer is the means whereby we let the Spirit of God breathe in and through us."[2] Breath, which is so integral to the fundamentals of movement, can be a physical metaphor for God breathing the Spirit in us. In turn, our exhalation can be symbolic of our response to the Spirit in our lives.

The biblical view, so apparent in the Old Testament and in the Hebrew understanding of the body, does not view the body as a series of unconnected parts. The Hebrews regarded the person as a totality: Body can be spirit, and spirit can be body. This does not mean that the Israelites did not differentiate between various aspects of an individual, but that human beings operate as integrated, connected, and embodied people. Body affects soul, soul affects body, heart affects body, body affects heart. Nowhere is this more apparent than in the terminology used and interchanged for the Hebrew words *heart, breath, soul, flesh, bones,* etc. We see a language that is bodily and gutsy, one where the flesh can thirst, the breath can praise, the bowels can think, the liver can lament, and the bones can proclaim, rejoice, and tremble. Body parts are constantly used to express the innermost yearnings and desires, the heartfelt prayer to God. What is felt in the soul and heart is expressed through the body.

Many translations of our Bibles prefer to translate

these references to body parts as either *heart, spirit, mind,* or *soul.* It is often only as we look to the Hebrew translation of the text that we see an immediate relationship between these parts. Let's reflect on a few examples from some of these texts and recapture some of the ways biblical authors flesh out the nuances of body-soul language in their laments and joys.

First, let us look at some of the ways the word *bones* are rendered. The primary association one often makes with the bones is that they break, and they are usually seen as the skeleton of our frames. The psalmist has a much broader association with the bones, equating them with the entirety of the heart and mind. Thus he says, "All my bones shall say, 'O Lord; who is like you?'" (Ps 35:10). Job speaks of all his bones shaking as dread came upon him in Job 4:14. When Jeremiah speaks of his heart being crushed, he says, "My heart is crushed within me, all my bones shake" (Jer 23:9). The bones have the capacity to cry out with both joy and lament, expressing our innermost states.

Other body parts reflect this relationship as well. Jeremiah cries out with his bowels, "My bowels, my bowels! I writhe in pain! Oh, the walls of my heart!" (Jer 4:19.)[3] The bowels not only express terror, but also compassion. In Jeremiah 31:20, the Lord speaks concerning Ephraim, saying, "My bowels groan for Ephraim; I will surely have mercy on him." Mercy comes from the very depths, from the bowels of God.

When someone laments, we do not see grief in the head but full bodily grief. The psalmist says, "For we sink down to the dust; our bellies cling to the ground" (Ps

44:25). And again, "My eye wastes away from grief, my soul and belly also" (Ps 31:9). The author of Lamentations says, "My eyes are spent with weeping; my liver churns" (Lam 2:11). The depths of the feelings of grief are fleshed out in the center of the torso: the belly and liver.

These are only a few examples, but one can find references to all the parts of the body as expression of an inward reality, including the head, face, nostrils, kidneys, heart, hands, or the entire flesh. The flesh that the Church has often associated with something evil is the very thing that sings for joy and longs for God.[4]

My soul longs, indeed it faints
for the courts of the Lord;
my heart and my *flesh* [emphasis mine] sing for joy
to the living God!

(Ps 84:2)

O God, you are my God, I seek you,
my soul thirsts for you;
my *flesh* faints for you,
as in a dry and weary land where there is no water.

(Ps 63:1)

Here we do not see a strict contrast between flesh, heart, kidneys, bones, or breath. All parts of the body can rejoice, all can lament, all express the longings of the human being. As voiced by J. Pedersen:

The soul is not a closely defined whole. It is a force, acting through all its parts. The whole of the soul

is in the reins, in the heart, in the flesh, just as, on
the other hand, the flesh stamps the whole of the
character of the soul.[5]

The anthropology of the body seen in the Old Testament reveals a close relationship between the soul and
the body in Hebrew thought. This is the heritage in the
Scriptures of the Old Testament and extended out in
the incarnation of Jesus Christ. God did not come to
bring salvation to only the soul, a concept that is so often
articulated in our inadequate language, but to bring redemption to the whole person: body and soul. The word
for salvation, *sozo,* as translated in the New Testament, is
sometimes rendered as *save,* and sometimes rendered as
healing. Sozo is used sixteen times in the synoptic[6] gospels
to tell of Jesus healing people in his midst. This is not
to make a theological statement on healing but rather to
show that God is concerned with the physical dimension.
Salvation is something that not only touches the soul
but touches the whole person. God is concerned with
spiritual *and* physical reality. They cannot be separated.
We are not only flesh, or bone, or breath. God intentionally made us as breathing-flesh, breathing-spirit. The
biblical text affirms that we were masterfully designed
as complete and complex organisms — the physical and
spiritual intertwined.
    Our language today can betray us when we speak
of the wonder of the human body. Even in our artic-
ulations about the body we dichotomize by constantly
separating the *body, heart,* or *soul.* This supports dualism and encourages the idea that we are unconnected.

The body is never just a body without spirit, nor is the mind separated from the body; mind and spirit are part of the body. It would be more accurate to call our-selves body-soul or body-spirit. The Hebrew tradition captures this in its rendering of different body parts cry-ing out to God. The Hebrews' language of the body has influenced my own language as I speak of the body, re-ferring even to "praying with the bones." I recognize that I, too, am caught in language. So if I speak at one point of the body and at another of the heart, it's because I want to convey they are deeply connected and dependent on one another, functioning as a whole organism.

A metaphor that is helpful in describing this integral connection between body and spirit is that of warp and weft in weaving. As you may recall, the warp threads run horizontally on the weaving and the weft run vertically. Both are needed to complete the weaving; they can be spoken of as separate, yet the weaving can only "be" a weaving if the warp and weft are both there. The psalmist in Psalm 139 speaks of the artistry of our Creator-Weaver weaving us into precious form. Who could compare to God and weave the body-spirit? We have been created by a proficient artist, and the finest architect or biologist cannot duplicate what God has created.

For you created my inmost being;
you knit me together in my mother's womb. . . .
My frame was not hidden from you
when I was made in the secret place.

When I was woven together in the depths of the earth,
your eyes saw my unformed body.

                                          (Ps 139:13, 15, NIV)

The Hebrew word for *woven* reveals an intricate process accomplished by the weaver; one that only the most skilled craftsperson could engage in.[7] God has woven bones, muscles, ligaments, organs, and life-giving blood together in the framework of fingers, legs, faces, torsos, and organs. Nowhere have I seen this more clearly than when my twin babies were growing within my womb. My weekly ultrasound would allow me to behold in duplicate tiny fingers, bones, spines, organs, heads, and faces all being woven into life. The miracle of life was being formed in my womb-studio. My babies were being shaped, embroidered, and woven with the care and complexity of the finest craftsperson. It was God's delight to give us life through a body and ultimately come to us in a body. The body was not an afterthought but part of intentional design.

The paradox of our bodies is that they are also fragile, like the consistency of clay. Clay can be broken and cracked, just as bones can be sprained and fractured. Bodies succumb to everyday annoyances of colds, stress, fatigue, and disease. Many have witnessed the painful reality of long-term illness, cancer, emotional illness, or AIDS. Our bodies are not perfect; neither are our hearts. The body can be a spiritual reminder of brokenness, our constant need for the One who created us.

As humans we find it very difficult to put the body, soul, mind, and heart in balance. At times we emphasize the body to the point of neglecting the heart. Physical exercise and toning can never ultimately bring about toning of the spiritual life, and neglect of the body can wreak havoc with the wholeness that God intended for us. We divide ourselves as if we were two complete organisms, one not affected by the other. Western culture is bombarded with images from the media that reveal a fragmented attitude toward the body. Often only segments of the body are depicted: chests, thighs, and posteriors are viewed as if there were no heads or hearts to accompany them. The perfect body image, communicated through TV, commercials, newspapers, billboards, and magazines, leads our culture to believe that the outer appearance of the body is of the most primary concern. Nothing could be further from the truth, and the body has become merely a well-designed tool for advertising. The image presented by the media has seeped its way into core attitudes toward the body, toward personal self-concept, and ultimately toward how we relate to each other and God. These attitudes are nothing new but have been an ongoing theme in Western culture for centuries. They may take different forms during different historical periods, but the consequence is the same: a dualistic philosophy in which body and soul are disconnected. Or, even worse, is what I would call "hierarchical dualism," where the physical or spiritual attributes of the body are positioned over one another. For example, the soul has been elevated over the body, so that anything to do with the soul, mind, or heart is worthwhile, and anything to do with the body is inferior and possibly evil.

Dualistic Thinking and the Body

Much of Western philosophy has been built upon the dualisms of spirit against matter, soul against body, sacred against profane.[8] Going back as far as Plato, we are told that the body is the "prison" of the soul and defiles the soul, inhibiting the soul's ability to know the divine. Therefore the soul yearns to be released from its captivity in the body.[9] The metaphor of the prison for the body supports the idea that we cannot know anything of "truth" through the body, that our feelings have no connection to our bodies. Descartes has said, "The soul by which I am what I am, is entirely distinct from body."[10] The body was seen only as something that was a hindrance. I believe the true "prison" of our bodies is *not* the body but the attitudes we hold concerning the body. The faulty premise of dualistic thinking prevents us from living out the reality of an "embodied people."

In classical Greek thought the body was equated with irrationality and had no capacity for rational discourse. The body was thought to only get in the way of pursuing knowledge, truth, or the greater things in life. In Plato's *Apology* this understanding is prevalent. In one dialogue Socrates is asking Simmias of the absolutes: Justice, Beauty, Goodness, Greatness, Strength — basically the true nature of everything. Socrates says, "Has the reality of these things ever been perceived by you through the bodily organs?" Listen to Simmias' reply:

And he attains to the knowledge of them in their
highest purity who goes to each of them with the

mind alone, not allowing when in the act of thought the intrusion or introduction of sight or any other sense in the company of reason, but with the very light of the mind in her clearness penetrates into the very light of truth in each; he has got rid, as far as he can, of eyes and ears and of the whole body, which he conceives of only as a disturbing element, hindering the soul from acquisition of knowledge when in company with her — is not this the sort of man who, if ever man did, is likely to attain the knowledge of existence?[11]

In Simmias' response there is the same attitude that has dominated both secular culture and the Church for ages: The body cannot be an avenue for pursuing knowledge, truth, or anything of the divine. Neoplatonic philosophers echo this as well; Plotinus, the Neoplatonic philosopher, spoke of the soul being "deeply infected with the taint of the body" and the soul actually being evil by being interfused with the body and by coming to share the body's states and to think the body's thoughts.[12] We are only left to wait in holy anticipation to be rid of this garment of disaster. Platonic and Neoplatonic dualism created a perfect setup for the continued dualisms in other points in history, the Enlightenment, and in the present age. The idea that the body can be part of the pursuit of wisdom or truth is antithetical to these philosophical frameworks. We are left, then, alienated from our bodies — the very dilemma from which Christ wanted to save us.

It is important to note that dualistic thinking was

part of the intellectual climate of the early Church. Many Church leaders were influenced by dualism, as Greek philosophy was a training ground for Church leaders. Scripture was eventually read through "the dualistic world view glasses."[13] The great leaders of the faith such as Clement, Origen, Augustine, and Aquinas inherited the legacy of dualistic thinking. This would influence not only the Church's view of the body for many centuries to come, but New Testament interpretation as well. Thankfully today biblical scholarship recognizes the importance of the bodily character of human nature, and in turn many churches and denominations are interested in including the body in the dimension of faith.

This does not mean that Greek philosophy, and in particular Plato and the Neoplatonists, have nothing to teach us; on the contrary, there is much to be learned from and inspired by their writings. It would be foolish to minimize the importance and magnitude of their contribution to philosophical thought as well as their influence on the arts. However, the way the notion of *dualism* has been interpreted throughout the ages by other theologians and philosophers has had a formidable effect on attitudes toward the body.

Dualistic thinking is still one of the main philosophical frameworks that hinders the human being from being at home with his/her body. We Westerners have taken a real blow and have been the ones who have lost out, becoming a fragmented people. It is time to take the body back from dualistic thinking, which is not a biblical model, as we will see in later chapters. Nor is it a model that honors the workmanship of the Creator; God is not honored in such thinking, for ultimately it tells God the way we were made was not good. When we say, "The body is bad," we challenge the truth that God saw creation and said, "It is very good."[14] We have idolized the spiritual, or immaterial, and frowned upon the earthy and material. This is idolatry — we worship our own image of our bodies, one that is unconnected to our souls, minds, and hearts. It is as if the painting could say to the artist, "I am not really a painting of those mountains. I really cannot be because all I am is tubes of paint on a canvas." The paint, canvas, and elements of design all work together to express the painter's vision of that mountain. They cannot be separated, and neither can we. God designed us to work together as a unity. Our bodies are not containers for our souls, minds, or hearts. Our minds and hearts are our bodies. Our bodies are our minds and hearts.

No matter how we say it, we have experienced a division or split between body and soul. Whether we elevate the body or denigrate the body, we run the risk of becoming a divided and fragmented people. When the body is elevated, people constantly strive for the perfect image. Internalizing who they are through the exterior, people inevitably come to the point where they hate their bodies, emotionally "beating up" on them because they never rise to their own expectations. If we denigrate the body, we again run the risk of not understanding its importance in our lives. In each scenario we end up feeling "un-at-home" with our bodies, and they become the prison Plato spoke of.

Honoring Our Body

God said, "I saw all that I made and it is very good."
(Gen 1:31)

These words come back to remind us that God is the author of our bodies. When we do not regard them with honor, we do not glorify the Creator. We in turn say the way we were made was not good, challenging God. Our bodies are a mark of our humanity. Our humanity is nothing to be ashamed of. It allows us to be beautiful and ugly, rough and smooth, frightened and calm. God loves it all, and we embody it all in body and soul. Our bodies can be a place where we celebrate our humanity and receive it as a gift from God.

What does it really mean to "honor our body"? This is a concept that we have finally owned when it comes to the environment or in how to take care of the body; what we feed it, how we clothe it, and how we treat it for medical problems. But inwardly our attitudes continue to disrespect it. We have not learned to be gentle with the body, listening to how it speaks. Honoring our body includes developing a different model for the way we perceive the body. We must continue to go back to the truth that God is the author of the body.

Yet God saw all that he had made and it was very good. God did not distinguish between making our hearts and bodies, but made us as *whole* individuals.

The biblical concept of the body is one that does not separate body and soul. It constantly affirms our interconnection, a beautiful weaving that God has made with warp and weft, using different colors, hues, shapes, and textures. We honor God and honor ourselves when we affirm the goodness and wholesomeness of God's creation in us. As we begin to use our bodies and souls in our very deepest expression, prayers, and yearnings, we affirm the wonder of the Creation story with all of our beings. We say "yes" at the deepest place that we were created an embodied people!

Notes

1. See J. Pedersen, *Israel: Its Life and Culture* (London: Oxford University Press, Vol. 1), pp. 99, 171.

2. Nancy Roth, *The Breath of God: An Approach to Prayer* (Cambridge, Mass.: Cowley Publications, 1990), p. 20.

3. I have used the NRSV translation but substituted the literal Hebrew translation here for *bowels*. The NRSV translates bowels as, "My anguish, my anguish! I writhe in pain." I have done this in other places where it concerns a specific body part and is translated with some other word.

4. For a more comprehensive study of the meaning of *flesh* in the Old and New Testaments see "Flesh" by A. C. Thiselton in Colin Brown, ed., *The New Dictionary of New Testament Theology*, Vol. 1 (Grand Rapids, Mich.: Zondervan Publishing House, 1979), pp. 671–82.

5. Pedersen, p. 178.

6. The synoptic gospels are the gospels of Matthew, Mark, and Luke.

7. The Hebrew word *raqam* is used in Ps 139:15 to designate the word *woven*. This refers to the same weaving process used for making the priestly garments (Ex 38:23, 35:25). This procedure was comprised of an intricate process using variegated blue, scarlet, and purple yarns in a sophisticated craft of embroidery and weaving. For a more thorough explanation of the weaving process see J. I. Packer, Merrill C. Tenney, William

White, Jr., *The Bible Almanac* (Nashville, Tenn.: Thomas Nelson Publishers, 1980), pp. 478–79.

8. For a more comprehensive understanding of the effect of dualism and the imagination on Western thinking see Richard Kearney, *The Wake of the Imagination* (Minneapolis, Minn.: University of Minnesota Press, 1988) p. 108.

9. See Brian Walsh, *Transforming Vision*, p. 66.

10. Descartes in Davies, p. 101.

11. Plato, *The Apology, Phaedo and Crito of Plato*, ed. Charles W. Elliot, LL.D., trans. Benjamin Jowett (Danbury, Conn.: Grolier Enterprises Corp., 1907, 1937, 1980), p. 54.

12. Plotinus in Davies, p. 86.

13. Walsh, p. 109.

14. See Genesis 2:31.

Chapter 3

THE INCARNATION

God and the Body

In the beginning was the Word, and the Word was with God, and the Word was God. The Word was with God in the beginning...The Word became flesh and dwelt among us.

These potent words from the first chapter of the Gospel of John poetically proclaim the spine of the Christian faith. God became human and made a home among us: living, breathing, eating, celebrating, and mourning with women, men, and children. Divinity became humanity in the incarnation of Jesus Christ. God chose to come in a body to express the fullness of love. God could have appeared through some amorphous vapor, or something even more spectacular, but no! God became known through human flesh, breathing and pulsing with all the limitations and capabilities we, as men and women, have, miracle and mystery twined together. God meets us in humanity, and we meet divinity.

This should not be surprising when we reflect on the ways God has used bodily imagery within the Old Testament to convey the fullness of mercy and love. The depths of God's tenderness are revealed through metaphors that have a bodily function, particularly metaphors of birth. The intensity of God's suffering love is compared to a woman in childbirth.

> For a long time I have kept silent,
> I have been quiet and held myself back.
> But now, like a woman in childbirth,
> I cry out, I gasp and pant. (Isa 42:14, NIV)

Several chapters later in the book of Isaiah we see God conveying deep caring for us in the comparison of giving birth.

> Listen to me, O house of Jacob, all you who remain of the house of Israel, you whom I have upheld since you were conceived, and have carried since your birth. Even to your old age and grey hairs I am the one who will sustain you. I have made you and I will carry you; I will sustain you and I will rescue you. (Isa 46:3–4)

God's love for humanity is seen in a bodily love. Nowhere is this more evident than in one of the words used in the Hebrew of the Old Testament for mercy and compassion. The same root used for mercy, *raham,* is also used for the word *womb.*

I will be gracious to whom I will be gracious, and will show mercy [*raham*] on whom I will show mercy." (Ex 33:19)

Before I formed you in the womb [*raham*] I knew you, before you were born I set you apart; I appointed you as a prophet to the nations. (Jer 1:5)

God shows womb-love, a love that is embedded in the body, earthy and divine, the love of a mother and the love of a father. Womb-love is a love that no force can break or alter; likened to the natural bond of a child in the womb, it is a strong love rooted in the body, soul, heart, and mind. It is mercy and compassion linked to the most intimate of experiences: bearing a child within the womb.

These are only a few illustrations of the way God can reveal love to us through bodily metaphor. Many of these metaphors can be wonderful starting points for reflection and meditation on God's bodily love and commitment to us.[1]

The incarnation of Jesus Christ is the culmination of bodily love, revealed in Yahweh of the Old Testament. Jesus continues to love with the nurturing images of the birthmother/birthfather.

O Jerusalem, Jerusalem, you who kill the prophets and stone those sent to you, how often I have longed to gather your children together, as a hen gathers her chicks under her wings, but you were not willing. (Mt 23:37)

Jesus comes to us in the entirety of what being human means, and his body is integral to both his humanity and his divinity. Jesus' vocation on earth came through his body: pounding nails, walking among the poor and brokenhearted, praying, kneeling, eating, washing feet, healing the sick. Jesus' hands became a living extension of the heart of God; his bodily touch was central to loving and healing people while on earth. Born into a culture that honored the body as an expression of the heart, Jesus would have had to walk, skip, run, jump, kneel, extend hands in prayer, and even dance!

But what is most important is not that Jesus kneeled or danced and that we should follow his example, but that God chose to be revealed through human flesh, through the physical, the body. This is stated so well by C. S. Lewis:

> Christianity is almost the only one of the great religions which thoroughly approves of the body — which believes that matter is good, that God himself once took on a human body, that some kind of body is going to be given to us even in Heaven and is going to be an essential part of our happiness, our beauty, and our energy.[2]

Those of us who struggle with our bodies, and most of us do in some form, must continue to be drawn back to the centrality that Christianity is an *incarnational* faith. The very fact of the incarnation *affirms* the body, not as something separate in and of itself, but as part of God's intentional design. We are our bodies, and if God can honor the body enough to be revealed through flesh, we need to take the body seriously.

At different times in history the Church has focused on either the divinity or humanity of Christ. Focusing on one and neglecting the other robs us of knowing part of who God is and ultimately of knowing ourselves as well. For example, if we see Jesus only as divine, we, too, easily miss the importance of our own bodies in the journey of the spiritual life. If we see only the humanity of Christ, we miss that communion with the Divine for which our hearts deeply hunger. It is part of human nature to emphasize one theological aspect in lieu of another. We must continue to be careful to keep in balance both humanity and divinity within the person of Jesus Christ. The words of Saint John of Damascus in the eighth century during the iconoclastic controversy, the controversy over visual images being used in worship, continue to speak to us today in considering this delicate balance:

> In former times God, who is without form or body, could never be depicted. But now when God is seen in the flesh conversing with men, I make an image of the god whom I see. I do not worship matter; I worship the Creator of matter who became matter for my sake, who willed to take His abode in matter; who worked out my salvation through matter. Never will I cease honoring the matter which wrought my salvation! I honor it but not as God.[3]

Humanity and divinity live together in Christ and cannot be separated. The fact that divinity and humanity can live together in community is witness of the miraculous.

Embracing Our Limitations

The incarnation beckons us to make friends with the reality of our bodies — to humbly accept our dwellings of clay. I often think of the image spoken of in Paul's letter to the Corinthians, which states that we have treasures in jars of clay (2 Cor 4:7).

> But we have this treasure in jars of clay to show that this all-surpassing power is from God and not from us.

I often feel as if I am a clay vessel, needing molding and forming, sometimes flexible and other times fragile and easily broken. I am very aware of my limitations, particularly through my body. Much of my daily work is dependent on my body, as mother, dancer, educator, and writer. As a mother, my love is extended through the physicality of breastfeeding, rocking, cuddling, holding, wrestling, nurturing, and playing with my children. Everyday gestures become gestures of loving prayer as I walk through each day. The demands of parenting and sometimes interrupted sleep mean I often enter a day physically tired, more than aware of my bodily limitations.

As a dancer, I also experience the limitations of my body. Warming up my muscles and ligaments does not always feel smooth and easy, and my body fights the discipline. But I can work only with what I have. If we do not work with limitations, we will never work at all. God coming in the incarnation is a story of divinity working through limitations. My body's limitations can be a place where grace is poured out, divinity meeting humanity.

The majority of my work as an educator is working with adults in various professions who have limited or no experience in dance or movement. Occasionally I work with trained or professional dancers, but this is not the norm. I do work with many adults who have always longed to move, aching to free their bodies in physical expression. Many remember dancing as a child and somehow looking back at this with great nostalgia. Questions that I am constantly asked are: "Can I really move and learn to use my body in expression of faith?" "I feel so awkward and ungraceful, how can I move?" It is not uncommon to see people apologizing for their lack of experience, something that needs no apology. Yet I see these same people moving in incredible and creative ways before God, welcoming their bodies to the process of spiritual growth. God works through the limitations of our bodies, whatever our shape or size, gender or cultural heritage, experience or lack thereof.

The incarnation gives me the grace to accept my limitations. Many times I am all too easily frustrated by the restrictions of my body in terms of endurance and technique — I must come to the reality of the incarnation daily. This is not an excuse for lack of application, skill, or desire to do the best I can; it is an invitation to risk. Risk often lies at the heart of calling back our bodies, to befriend them again as we did when we were children.

Risk also lies at the core of incarnation. For God to become human was a mission in uncompromising risk. Jesus lived risk in every way; in fact he surrendered to becoming despised, rejected, and a fool for the sake of love. Incarnation was and is dangerous. Pain was at the heart of Jesus' birth, life, and death. There is pain in the kind of love that is womb-love; the pangs of labor bring forth the miracle of life from the womb. God's birthing Jesus to us was a risk. We in turn are invited on a journey to risk in the life of faith. Including our bodies on that journey is a deeper invitation to risk. My mother once told me, "Celeste, the depth of your suffering will equal the depth of your joy." I have often thought of this in reflecting on the invitation to risk. The more I risk, the more I can fully experience life — both the pain and the joy. The incarnation gives us solid ground to risk with our bodies in the spiritual journey.

During a class I teach on embodied prayer, I often give an assignment to do a simple gesture prayer or circle dance to a hymn, chorus, or prayer, something that the students can teach the entire class. In this way the whole class is able to participate and incorporate many people's body prayers, that are beautiful ways to pray. The "Jesus Prayer" is an ancient prayer from the Russian Orthodox Christian tradition that is repeated many times, meditatively, quietly, till it becomes like breath. It is an invitation to prayer that can be done throughout the day, whether in the midst of busyness or in the quiet of solitude. It is simply, "Lord, Jesus Christ, have mercy on me a sinner." One particular time, as one of my students showed us her simple yet expressive gestures to this prayer, I found the words reaching a deep place inside me. For the first time this prayer reached my total body. As I stretched my arms firmly in the air, I communicated to God with all of my being that I was truly thirsty, and I became ready to receive the mercy of God through my body. Since I prayed this prayer through my body, it has been incarnated in me in a new way. I had prayed the "Jesus Prayer" for years, but now as I pray it verbally, I am always reminded of those clear images of bodies reaching and stretching for God's mercy and receiving mercy in a simple gathering motion with the humility of body gestures.

Embracing the Wonder

At the same time that we need to embrace our limitations, we must also embrace the wonder of our bodies. Our bodies may not be exactly the way we would like; but let us ponder for a moment the way we were created. No artist could form us with such precision and mastery as the Creator-Artist. Vincent Van Gogh, the famous painter, recognized this with clarity:

Christ alone . . . lived serenely as a greater artist than all other artists, despising marble and clay as well as color, working in living flesh. That is to say, this matchless artist, hardly to be conceived of by the

obtuse instrument of our modern, nervous, stupe-
fied brains, made neither statues nor pictures nor
books; he loudly proclaimed that he made . . . living
men [women], immortals.[4]

Our lives are formed by an incredible artist with a
capital *A!* We have seen and heard so much about the
"perfect body" that we have forgotten the sheer wonder of toenails, noses, muscles, fingers, hair, and knees.
Martha Graham, a pioneer in modern dance, recognizes
this same truth:

The next time you look into the mirror, just look at
the way the ears rest next to the head; look at the
way the hairline grows; think of all the little bones
in your wrist. It is a miracle. And the dance is a
celebration of that miracle.[5]

The body is truly a miracle. We must again come and see
the beauty lying within each of us. To pray with our bodies is an affirmation of that miracle. An affirmation to
the Creator that yes, we want to participate with God in
this exciting, beautiful, and even painful journey we call
life. I believe that one of the most important elements in
befriending our bodies and healing the division between
body and soul is to bring them into the life of prayer. As
we do this, we become whole. The incarnation is our invitation to become whole; it renews the view of our bodies
as a sacred place for dialogue with God, with each other,
and with ourselves.

Notes

1. For resources in using the feminine in metaphors, prayer, and reflection see Kathleen Fischer, *Women at the Well: Feminist Perspective on Spiritual Direction* (New York: Paulist Press, 1988) and Virginia Ann Froehle, R.S.M, *Called Into Her Presence: Praying with Feminine Images of God* (Notre Dame, Ind.: Ave Maria Press, 1992).

2. C. S. Lewis, *Mere Christianity* (New York: Macmillan Publishing Co., 1943), p. 91.

3. St. John of Damascus, *St. John of Damascus on the Divine Images: Three Apologies Against Those Who Attack the Divine Images,* trans. David Anderson (Crestwood, N.Y.: St. Vladimir's Seminary Press, 1980), p. 23.

4. Vincent Van Gogh, *Van Gogh: A Self Portrait: Letters Revealing His Life As a Painter,* selected by W. H. Auden (Greenwich, Conn.: New York Graphic Society, 1961), p. 302.

5. Martha Graham, *Blood Memory* (New York: Doubleday, 1991), p. 5.

Chapter 4

METAPHOR AND SPIRITUALITY

 ∾

The sacred does not always take shape in clear, rational formulas, or in predictable experiences. Rather, the sacred is concerned with otherness and mystery. God comes to us in metaphor, linking the visible with the invisible, spirit with matter. Pure theological discourse cannot explain the mystery of the Trinity, the wonder of the Incarnation, or the appearance of God in a burning bush. God speaks to us through metaphorical language: language where one thing is likened to another. The biblical writers consistently use metaphor as a way of giving us a glimpse of who God is. God is like a potter, and we are the clay (Is 45:9; 64:8; Jer 18). God is like a midwife (Ps 22:9) and also like a rock (Ps 18:2). God is like a shield around one's head (Ps 3:3), and like one who has wings we can hide in (Ps 17:8). God comforts us the way a mother comforts a child (Is 66:13) and has compassion on us as a father has compassion on his children (Ps 103:3). God is a fortress (Ps 59, 62) and the one who thunders (Ps 29). These images do not declare that God is literally a potter, fortress, mother, father, eagle, shield, or rock. They tell us something of God's nature. God can have a fatherly love and motherly love. God can hide and protect us as an eagle with her eaglet or be a rock to firmly stand upon. We get a glimpse of the spiritual by its relationship to the earthly. The spiritual and physical become intertwined through metaphor, the sacred is given flesh.

The biblical writers also describe people's experience of God in metaphorical language. The one who meditates on God's Word is compared to a tree planted by streams of water (Ps 1). God makes our feet like the deer (Ps 18:33), and God's word is like a fire in Jeremiah's bones (Jer 20:9). Jesus continues in this tradition, likening himself to the vine, with God as the gardener and humankind as the branches (Jn 15). We are recognized by our fruit (Mt 7:17–20), and our eye is like the lamp of our body (Mt 6:22, Lk 11:34). The heart of Jesus' words is communicated through the eyes of an artful storyteller, allowing us to see, touch, and smell the kingdom of God. Jesus is truly a "metaphor maker," one who took the raw materials of everyday life and shaped them in parabolic language, opening us to the love of God. Our hearing and seeing lead to understanding and perceiving.[1]

God's Word can be transformative because of the way truth is made known. We are invited into the biblical text by the use of our imaginations and bodies, thus being able to bring our own stories and experiences into the text. The text therefore becomes "participatory," enabling us to bring our particular experiences and feel-

ings into the historical event. When Jesus says to us that
we are like the branches on a tree and he is a vine, we
can visualize this image. We are told to remain in the
vine so we can bear fruit. As we look at the maple out our
window, the oak on our grandfather's farm, or the grapes
in our friend's fruit orchard, we can remember through
our inner eye the importance of "remaining in the vine."
This image stays in our hearts, minds, and bodies more
than a theological discourse on the meaning of Christ.
When the wind is likened to the Spirit in the Gospel of
John, we get a real sense of how the Spirit acts in our life
through our experience of the wind. We complete the
parable by our own experience and are called into *active*
listening. As said so well by Belden Lane in his work on
Jesus' parables:

> A certain inconclusiveness is always basic to success
> of a metaphor. Jesus spoke in parables because he
> knew all language, but especially metaphor, to be a
> matter of masking as well as revealing. It forces the
> listener to work as well as the storyteller, not releas-
> ing its gifts until each have claimed responsibility
> for its completion.[2]

Metaphor uses the stuff of imagination; it both masks
and reveals. Metaphorical language is not found in the
visual images of TV, where everything is received on a
platter. Instead, it's through the medium of stories, poetry, visual art, dance, and song that we are given layers
of meaning to ponder. Our God-given imaginations are
enlivened, and we celebrate what C. S. Lewis calls "the

baptized imagination." Metaphors beckon us to listen to God with all of our senses and invite us to respond to the Holy in fullness.

The nature of metaphor is symbolic language, and symbol can take shape in words, clay, paint, sounds, fiber, or movement. The artist uses symbol and metaphor as the meat of his/her work. *Symbol* comes from the Greek *sym,* meaning *with* or *together,* and *bollein,* meaning *to throw* or *to draw.* Symbols basically bring together our human experience — we can dance our symbols, act our symbols, draw our symbols, or write our symbols. Symbols can be very ordinary actions as well, but nonetheless meaningful. A handshake, putting flowers on the table, bowing in prayer, or a photo on our fridge are all symbols that can make the ordinary extraordinary.

Wheat, wine, water, bread, and fruit are no longer only staples of life but take on symbolic spiritual significance through the eyes of Jesus. Jesus took ordinary matter to reveal the extraordinary. In other words, spirituality became earthy and accessible because it was communicated through the ordinary events of life: fishing, making bread, considering the lilies, finding a lost coin, or farming. If Jesus came in this century, we would no doubt have more metaphors to do with computer technology than with the vocation of farming. In each century we need to put the "old metaphors" into language that is meaningful for us today. The language of movement allows us to contemporize old metaphors and make them our own.

As people on a spiritual journey, we need symbol, metaphor, and ritual as ways to express the inexpressible. The twentieth-century visual artist Paul Klee said, "Art does not reproduce the visible; rather it makes visible."[3] Paul Klee was speaking in the context of the formal elements of abstract art, but the meaning can easily be carried over to the use of metaphor and symbol. Metaphors do not reproduce God, but rather they make God visible to us. With this understanding we are not as apt to idolize art or symbol, for art does not reproduce God but makes God more visible to our hearts and bodies. It points us to the Way.

As said so well by Gertrud Mueller Nelson in her book *To Dance With God:*

> This creative and poetic Church helps us to pay full attention to what we might otherwise deem ordinary and commonplace. Rites and symbols use the ordinary and earthy elements of our existence and, by encircling them, ratify, sanctify, complete. The ordinary becomes the container for the divine and safely holds what was uncontainable. The transcendent is disclosed in what is wonderfully familiar: bread, wine, fire, ash, earth, water, oil, tears, seeds, songs, feastings and fastings, pains and joys, bodies and thoughts, regressions and transformations. It draws its action more from what is most human in us than from theology. In its creative function, the Church speaks directly to the heart, a heart which hears symbols, not rational vocabulary.[4]

Movement Metaphors

Metaphorical language is gutsy and earthy, poetic and imaginative, and most of all bodily. As Nelson says, it takes that which is familiar to us. What could be more familiar to us than our bodies? So familiar, in fact, that we forget what a powerful metaphor our bodies can be. The invitation to bodily prayer is an invitation to pray the metaphors of Scripture through every fiber of our being. The metaphorical language of Scripture can be given shape in the expressive language of our bodies. When we express the biblical text through our bodies, we "get inside" the text in a whole new way and meet the Word of God in a deep place. Expressing the metaphors and images of Scripture through our bodies gives us the opportunity to grapple with the text personally and make it our own in a way that is printed indelibly upon our bones. Word becomes flesh as we allow our bodies to be a living metaphor of God's Word. Word is written on flesh in an act of incarnational prayer.

Our gestures, postures, expression, and creative movement can all be "movement metaphors,"[5] ways of communicating something else through the power of body language. Bowed heads, reaching arms, jumping feet, enclosed or open bodies, all become movement metaphors that reveal a deeper reality. Metaphors through words create a visual image in our imaginations. Translating those metaphors in our bodies fleshes out that image so we can see it and experience it in our bones.

The best way to experience this firsthand is to take a few lines of Scripture and begin to express them through your bodily expression, finding postures, gestures, and movements that communicate the "feel" of the text. It is not as if one needs to express every word through movement, but more to reach the essence or the kernel of truth in the text. Even as you read this book, you may want to take a five-minute break, find a Scripture that may be meaningful to you, and try to verbalize the words through the language of your gestures, motions, posture, and expressive movement. Allow your body to be an extension of the words as if you had only your movement to proclaim or pray this text. It could be as simple as praying in movement the familiar verses of Paul, "Brothers and sisters, by the mercies of God, present your bodies as a living sacrifice, holy and acceptable to God, which is your spiritual worship" (Rom 12:1). These verses, which you may have heard over and over again, may take on a new shape as you concretely offer all of your body to God. Notice how your body movement changes your reading of the text. What did you perhaps notice that you didn't notice before? Does the text relate to you in a more personal way?

In some ways our religious imaginations need to be healed from many of the stereotypical ways we perceive God. God breaks through every notion and cannot be contained by our limited imaginations. We need the Spirit to cultivate ways of hearing, seeing, and perceiving God that transcend our limited view. Scripture does this if we carefully look at the entire spectrum of metaphor that describes God. Unfortunately we have usually heard the same metaphors over and over again, forgetting some of the others. For example, I have predominantly heard the metaphor of God as judge, ruler, king, and warrior. Only in recent years have I personally reclaimed the biblical images of God as potter, weaver, eagle, or midwife. These other metaphors give me a more complete understanding of who God is and can be in my life.

Bringing our bodies to the life of faith allows us to begin to heal our imaginations. As Kathleen Fischer, spiritual director and writer, says, "The imagination is changed and healed when addressed in its own language, that is, in the concrete language of image, metaphor, and story."[6] Since God has addressed us in the language of metaphor, it only makes sense that we in turn address God and continue to listen to God through metaphor. Bringing our bodies to the process makes this a tangible reality.

Let me give some examples to demonstrate how movement can speak to us in our spiritual formation. Movement can be a point of entry into our own story and the story of God in our lives.

Listening to Our Own Metaphors

One of the exercises I repeatedly do in my workshops is a "rocking exercise." It is usually done after we warm up our bodies and have a chance to quietly reflect on God's nurturing love to us. I simply ask people to find a comfortable position where they can just rock, experiencing the gentle rhythms of rocking. This may be done lying on the floor holding knees to chests going from side to side, or it may be sitting up holding knees with the head tucked down. The position can be changed at any point as well. I often have my students reflect on being rocked and held in God's arms. A psalm that is helpful to meditate upon while doing this exercise is Psalm 131.

> But I have calmed and quieted my soul,
> like a weaned child with its mother;
> my soul is like the weaned child that is with me.
>
> (Ps 131:2)

One participant in a workshop, whom I will call Gail, shared a meaningful experience she had while doing this rocking exercise. While rocking, Gail had a strong image of being in the womb, possibly before birth, and of God's hand held directly under her tiny formed body. This was a very healing image, which illustrated the continuity of God's care for her since she began in the womb. She was profoundly moved by this image of God's love. So this simple exercise can give us a chance to experience movement that is very meaningful to us. Being rocked in God's arms becomes a prayer of receiving God's love. We often think of prayer as only "asking," but there is always the possibility for both receiving and asking, of an ongoing dialogue with the One who loves us.

I have spent ample time rocking my children. In the time I was forming much of the framework of this book, I was rocking my twin babies, who are now toddlers. As I rocked, I often imagined God rocking me. Tired and often drained of energy, I yearned to be rocked in the arms of God, just as I rocked my little ones. As I felt cherished again by God, I was energized to cherish others.

This basic metaphor of rocking is one that I think we could incorporate for the rest of our lives in our prayer. We need to feel in our bodies how precious it is to be still in the heart of God.

The "movement metaphor" of rocking becomes a link into our own faith story. Gail was able to deepen her experience of the love of God, even from the time she was in her mother's womb. My experience was a physical reminder that I was "a cherished one" as I gave to my two little ones all my love and energy. Movement metaphors can become points of entry into our own stories, and in our own stories we find the story of God. The sacred takes shape through the physical, and we are again named, cherished through the Beloved. We allow God to transform our hearts through the simple actions of rocking, bowing, dancing, or lifting hands. There is an old Hebrew proverb that says, "Put something where you can see it so your eye will remind your heart."[7] Movement reminds our eye so our heart will be reminded.

Movement As a Metaphor
for the Spiritual Journey

The life of prayer is not an activity that proceeds in a straight line. If any visual image would be communicative of prayer, it would not be an arrow always straight up, or a line constantly ascending. The life of prayer is characteristic of ups and downs, listening and asking, joy and lament. We have times of experiencing the presence of God and times of experiencing the absence of God.

There are days we may "feel" like praying and days we don't. We have seasons of feeling we are progressing on this spiritual journey and seasons when we are deeply discouraged. Taking our "spiritual temperature" at any one point can be dangerous; in fact, we can never accurately measure the spiritual life. There are days we want to move our bodies in the morning and days we don't. But we continue to move. We continue to pray, groaning in the dark and dancing in the light, pressing on in this wonderful and paradoxical journey.

Movement can be a metaphor for the spiritual journey. Movement consists of a wide variety of motions: rising, sinking, climbing, falling, skipping, walking, dancing, bending, stretching, returning, clinging, contracting, reaching, releasing, and holding. All of these movements, common to everyday life, are also what we do in the spiritual journey. We climb and we fall. We rise and we sink. We cling to God and we release to God. We stretch out to God and we retreat from God. We walk steadfast and we walk bent. We return, again and again. The life of faith is characterized by returning to God, returning to the center. Returning to listening to the Spirit. The theological term *repentance* literally means to return. Turning is a fundamental concept in dance. Many of us may enjoy just watching the classical ballet dancer do one pirouette after another. We turn and turn and turn. In faith we turn and turn. Turning to God. Turning to others. Turning to ourselves and from ourselves.

The life of prayer is one of movement. Our movement may comprise falling as well as getting up and dancing. Each posture is important to the life of prayer and part of the spiritual journey. We need to embrace our low points and our high points. If the dancer does not come to the ground, we cannot appreciate the time she rose to the heights. If the dancer did not turn, we would see him only two-dimensionally. Our faith is three-dimensional, and as we begin to pray through our bodies, we can embrace the many dimensions of faith.

Notes

1. See Celeste Schroeder, "Gestures of Proclamation," *Liturgy*, Vol. II, No. 1, Summer 1993, p. 66.

2. Belden Lane, "Language, Metaphor, and Pastoral Theology," *Theology Today* 42, No. 4 (Jan. 1987), 487–502.

3. Paul Klee in Herschel B. Chipp, *Theories of Modern Art: A Source Book by Artists and Critics* (Berkeley, Calif.: University of California Press, 1968), p. 182.

4. Gertrud Mueller Nelson, *To Dance With God: Family Ritual and Community Celebration* (New York: Paulist Press, 1986), p. 7.

5. *Movement metaphors* is a term I have phrased as a way of describing the symbolic nature of movement. *Movement metaphors* are thus what we make all the time when we use movement as an expressive language.

6. Kathleen Fischer, *Women At The Well: Feminist Perspectives on Spiritual Direction* (New York: Paulist Press, 1988), p. 65.

7. I am indebted to Martha Zimmerman, who has often shared this quote in her own teaching and writing.

Part Two

LEGACY OF EMBODIED PRAYER

Chapter 5

PRAYING WITH THE BONES I
Old Testament

———————— ⧼ ————————

A reading of the Old Testament through the eyes of a dancer captures a beautiful interweave between body and heart, body and soul. Leaping off the pages are historical encounters of men and women lifting hands in prayer, bowing and falling prostrate in God's presence, crouching and rolling with grief, and dancing with festive praise. The people of Israel are a dancing people, a moving people, a people embodying all their glories and all their warts. Curt Sachs, a dance historian, has said there are "few danceless peoples." Dance is integral to the fabric of most cultures, and some more than others. If any people could be described as "a dancing people," it would be the men and women of the Old Testament.[1]

In the Old Testament theology is transformed to doxology, and a bodily one at that. Adam and Eve walk with God in the garden, Solomon spreads his hands in prayer, Miriam dances when God parts the Red Sea,

Daniel falls prostrate in deep reverence, Jeremiah clings to the ground with his belly, and David dances vigorously in procession with the ark. These bodily actions suggest a transparency to God, both in the body and the heart. These people were unashamed to present all of themselves to God.

The Old Testament is rich in bodily expression: posture, gesture, dance, and dramatic expression are woven into the text. Even more startling are the varied colors of this tapestry of movement. We do not have postures only in colors of blue, but red, yellow, black, white, and purple. Room is given for expressing the full dimension of the body-soul, from grieving to rejoicing, from humility to anger, from reverence to jubilation. Prayer is not only petition, but becomes adoration, confession, supplication, praise, and lament — all lived out through bodily expression. Together they give us an example of weaving the spiritual and earthly life together, making body and soul one.

Unfortunately the Church today often has room only for gestures of reverence, *or* gestures of joy, both not being visible in the same tradition. For example, it is encouraged in some churches to kneel and other churches to dance with a tambourine. It is less usual to find a church where both postures are incorporated into the life of worship. The Hebrew tradition, however, gives us a more comprehensive model for practicing body prayer. There, the life of faith is multidimensional; all of who we are comes into the work of transformation.

The holistic anthropology evident in the Old Testament was lived out in the bodies of men and women.

It was not a philosophical or theological doctrine given only intellectual assent, but was breathed and danced out in the body-soul of the people. Many of us may believe in a nondualistic anthropology, found in the Old Testament, which attests that we are body-soul. Yet unless we have a pragmatic way of letting our philosophy reach our bodies, it may stay a tightly packaged philosophical framework in our head, never reaching the deeper part of us. So in essence we remain dualistic, supporting the very things we detest. The well-known poet W. B. Yeats has said, "We only believe those thoughts which have been conceived not in the brain but in the whole body."[2] The invitation to bodily prayer knocks dualism out of our bodies and allows us to live out what we really believe in our heads and hearts. The Hebrew people give us an incredible historical heritage from which to learn, glean, and jump off as we explore more fully what it means to be an embodied people.

In the life of the Israelites we see a God who dances with them and mourns with them. The little word *with* becomes very important in understanding our journey in prayer. God is with us — in our rising, sinking, clinging, lifting, and dancing prayers. When God reminds Joshua not to be frightened or discouraged when taking over the leadership of Israel after Moses' death, God gives Joshua great consolation. God's consolation is to tell Joshua over and over again, "I will be with you . . . I will never leave you nor forsake you."[3] We do not walk alone, but God is with us. We may not always "feel" God's presence in the darkness, lightness, or in-between, yet God is there in the dark and the light, and one is not always better than the other. Often in our darkness we can have more of a sense of God's "withness"; in our lightness we too easily carry ourselves in our own strength.

We cannot conjure up God by using our bodies, or by using some magical formula. God has taken the initiative to be with us. Even as we pray, the Spirit is within us and praying through us. God walks with us in our journey of bodily prayer, both in our falling and rising. Even though we may know God is with us in our heads, I believe it is when we risk letting God into our bodies that we can comprehend "withness" more completely.

God physically moved in history with the Israelites, as they were led out of Egypt. God went before the people of Israel in a cloud as they literally walked, grumbled, and grasped for manna in the desert. The idea of movement was fundamental to the Israelites; they may have not articulated it as such, but movement became a foundational metaphor for the spiritual journey: walking through the desert, dancing in praise, standing in prayer, or rolling in lament are integral to the spiritual-physical reality.

One chapter could hardly capture the enormity of the ways bodily movement is used within the Old Testament. Indeed, a book could be dedicated just to the way dance is used, or postures of lament. Other chapters in this book will refer back to the Old Testament as the seasons of embodied prayer are developed from lament to joy. Let us look at the overall weaving to get a clearer idea of some of the colors of posture.

The Postures of Prayer

Bowing and kneeling in God's presence were symbolic of humility and reverence.[4] Deep reverence for God was further shown in the act of falling prostrate.[5] Bowing, kneeling, or falling prostrate can remind us of the kind of God we have. It can be a physical reminder that God is beyond any of our gestures, postures, or preconceived ideas. God is Other, yet we are in communion with God. Transcendent and immanent. The posture of kneeling reminds us of the "mystery" of God, the "awesomeness" of God, the One who is the great I Am, the Maker of heaven and earth.

These postures reveal who God is to us. Even in the posture of Moses taking off his sandals at the burning bush, we see again a posture of awe. Moses doesn't bow, kneel, or fall prostrate but reveals a deep reverence with this posture. He stands on holy ground. Holy ground must be met with pure vulnerability. It calls for physical expression, beckoning us to take off our shoes and stand on holy ground when we pray with our bodies.

It is characteristic of modern dancers to dance in bare feet. A classical ballet dancer wears ballet shoes, or point shoes, a jazz dancer would wear jazz shoes, a tap dancer would wear tap shoes. I am primarily a modern dancer, so I usually dance barefooted. My bare feet are a reminder to me of the posture of Moses, taking his shoes off on holy ground. As I dance in a variety of sanctuaries, I am reminded that I am on holy ground, not because I am in the physical place of a church, but because God is present in our midst. I come with a posture of awe, in my dance of jubilation and in my dance of lament.

If we have been exposed only to postures of kneeling or bowing, we may not find these postures as meaningful. They may have become too rote for us, and we may need a season to explore other forms of bodily prayer such as extended hands, clenched fingers, or reaching torsos. It is a grave mistake to express only one kind of posture in prayer through the entirety of our earthly spiritual life. We can easily acquire a distorted view of God. We may have reverence but lose the postures of jubilation, intimacy, surprise, or lament. We then see only one side of God, and therefore our relationship with God can lack the intimacy of real communion. However, without any postures of reverence we might miss out on a big part of who God is. We need a variety of postures of prayer to express a full-orbed life with God.

The people of the Old Testament lived this out as they cried out to God with not only bowed heads, but with extended, raised, or lifted hands. For example, when Solomon gives a prayer of dedication for the temple, he kneels before the whole assembly of Israel and "spreads out his hands in prayer." The psalmist reveals the relationship between praise and lifting up hands, exclaiming, "I will praise you as long as I live, and in your name I will lift up my hands" (Ps 63:4). The very act of lifting up our hands extends our hearts and bodies to God. Whether with a heart of prayer, or gesture of praise, we reach as far as we can to the heart of God. Our bodies say Yes to God! Yes to life! In our reaching and stretching we stretch to our Maker, and our Maker bends to us. We become released and freed as we extend our hands to God. In this simple posture we surrender to the mystery of the One who made us. We come wanting to receive, and we leave full.

The prayer of lament became associated with crouching and rolling movements, so characterized in the psalmist's words, "We are brought down to the dust; our bodies cling to the ground." Their bellies literally contracted with the pain of grief, which became the prayer of lament. When we give expression to lament, it does not fester in our body as a sore wound. The active experience of grief gives us the courage to go on to the path of transformation. Painful as it is to attend to our shortcomings, griefs, or disappointments, our bodies need to express out of the depths, and we need to begin to see even our laments as prayer. This is dealt with in detail in the chapter on lament.

Dance As a Posture of Joy

Dance in the Old Testament became a response of the worshiping heart. The Hebrews' worship could not be contained in their heads but had to reach every fiber of their bodies, fulfilling that well-known command to love God with all your heart, soul, and strength.[6] Their dance was characterized by motions of spontaneous praise and worship, a prayer of thanksgiving for what God had done in their lives. It was not a rehearsed step-by-step dance, but a dance that swept their thanksgiving into their fingers and toes.

Dancing was so integral to Hebrew culture that there are numerous words for *dance* used in the Bible.[7] Unfortunately the English texts only translate these words as *dance,* though the Hebrew articulates the nuances of these dance words and gives us an example of the kind of dance that was done. Words are used such as *skip, whirl, rotate, leap, dance in a playful manner,* or *dance in a circle.* For example, in the wonderful parallel passages where David is dancing in procession before the ark, the Old Testament uses five different Hebrew words to describe David's dance.[8]

> David danced before the Lord with all his might; David was girded with a linen ephod. So David and all the house of Israel brought up the ark of the Lord with shouting, and with the sound of the trumpet. As the ark of the Lord came into the city of David, Michal daughter of Saul looked out of the window, and saw King David leaping and dancing before the Lord; and she despised him in her heart ... [David replies later to Michal]. "It was before the Lord, who chose me in place of your father and all his household, to appoint me as prince over Israel, the people of the Lord, that I have danced before the Lord." (2 Sam 6:14–16, 21)

The Hebrew verbs meaning *to dance* literally tell us that David skipped, danced in the ordinary sense, playfully danced, rotated with all his might, or whirled continually. I enjoy hearing the nuances of how David danced because it tells me something of the spirit of his dance and captures a vigor and abandonment in his worship that can be somewhat lost in the English translation. The variety of Hebrew words used for *dance* supports the reality that dance was such an integral part of worship in Israelite culture that one word was not sufficient to describe the nuances of dance.

Dance was characterized by a *response* to God in worship. This was a different approach to dance in the geographic area, since dance in neighboring cultures was often utilized as a way to get to God, rather than a response to God. In neighboring cultures some of the functions of dance were a means of appeasing or awakening the gods, helping crops grow, or creating union with a deity by imitation.[9] An example of dance in the Old Testament in a neighboring culture is found in the book of Kings; the people dance around the altar trying to get the god Baal's attention (1 Kings 18:26). Egypt and Babylon both incorporated dance in part of their religious ceremony. A trip to a museum with Egyptian art will allow you to see postures of dance inscribed or painted on tomb paintings or vases. The people in the Old Testament were certainly influenced by the postures of dance in neighboring cultures, however they incorporated the form of the dance, rather than the function of how dance was used.

Dance in the Old Testament is characterized by a response of thanksgiving. So when we see God parting the Red Sea to assure safety for the Israelites, Miriam leads the women with tambourines and dancing to celebrate what God has done.[10] How appropriate! A miracle of that magnitude certainly calls for a full response, one of song, music, and dance. The people of Israel's prayers were answered, God brought victory to them, and the response is one of joyous worship and celebration.

There are numerous references to the uses of dance in the Old Testament.[11] Dance became so associated with joy that in some passages it is actually used as a metaphor for joy and as the opposite to mourning. As said by the author of Ecclesiastes, there is "a time to mourn, and a time to dance" (Eccles 3:4b). Or as the psalmist says, "You turned my wailing into dancing; you removed my sackcloth and clothed me with joy" (Ps 30:11–12, NIV). Yet even in their mourning, they danced a dance of lament. The heritage of the Old Testament gives us a people who strove to worship and pray with all of their being. God was not concerned with a particular movement, or even if they did move. God is concerned with a "broken spirit" more than falling on the ground and a "clean heart" more than outstretched arms.[12] Yet the testimony of bodily prayer in the Old Testament reveals to us that the Israelites had permission to use their bodies. They danced out of the depths and echo what Brother Robert of Taizé says: "Dance is a way of expressing the spiritual animation that swells from the depths of the human heart."[13] Their inner beings were written on their bodies, and they give us hope and strength to pursue being a people of embodied faith.

The Israelites give us an example of prayer meeting them in daily ritual, in petition and confession, praise and worship, feast time and mourning time. They knew, as David said when he danced, that they move "before"

God. It was not a performance but a bodily-soul offering to God. An offering of love. Their approach teaches us to move with reverence and awe, delight and surprise. To be open to the spontaneous and playful dimension of life. The Hebrews gave us a spirituality with physicality. We in turn are urged by the psalmist to "Let everything that breathes praise God!" (Ps 150:6)

Notes

1. Curt Sachs, *World History of the Dance* (New York: W. W. Norton & Company, 1937), p. 11.
2. W. B. Yeats in Charles Davis, *Body as Spirit: The Nature of Religious Feeling* (New York: Seabury, 1976), p. 11.
3. See Joshua, Chapter 1.
4. For a few examples see Psalms 5, 95, 136.
5. For example, see Daniel 8:17–18.
6. Deuteronomy 5:6.
7. For a thorough understanding of the Hebrew words used for dance see Mayer Gruber, "Ten Dance-Derived Expressions in the Hebrew Bible," *Biblica*, Vol. 62, 1981. This article is also reprinted in Doug Adams and Diane Apostolos-Cappadona, eds., *Dance as Religious Studies* (New York: Crossroad, 1990), pp. 48–66.
8. See 2 Samuel 6 and 1 Chronicles 15. The Hebrew words used here are *karar, pazaz, sahak, rakad,* and *hul.*
9. For a detailed description of the entire scope of sacred dance in other cultures see W. O. E. Oesterley, *The Sacred Dance: A Study in Comparative Folklore* (Cambridge, England: University Press, 1923).
10. See Exodus 15:20–21.
11. See Exodus 15:20, 32:19, Judges 11:34, 21:21–23, 1 Samuel 18:6–7, 21:11, 29:5, 2 Samuel 6:11–21, 1 Chronicles 15:29, 1 Kings 18:26, Song of Songs 6:13, Psalms 30:11–12, 149:3,

150:4, Lamentations 5:15, Jeremiah 31:4, 13, Job 21:11, Ecclesiastes 3:4.

    12. See Psalm 51:17 and Isaiah 1:15–16.

    13. Brother Robert of Taizé in Martin H. Blogg, *Time to Dance* (London: Collins Liturgical Publications, 1984), p. 52.

Chapter 6

PRAYING WITH THE BONES II

New Testament

&

The New Testament continues in the tradition of Hebrew culture: Bowing, standing, kneeling, lifting hands, laying on of hands, or falling on the ground are bodily postures that accompany prayer. The very act of bowing and lifting hands becomes a prayer in and of itself, a statement defining a relationship with the Beloved. This relationship is characterized by a vulnerable heart, a heart filled with humility and adoration. Paul tells us to lift up holy hands in prayer, and he urges us to kneel before God and pray.[1] We see Jesus kneeling in prayer; the Gospel of Matthew records him falling with his face to the ground while praying in Gethsemane.[2]

One of the words most frequently used for _prayer_ in the New Testament is the Greek word _proskyneo_, which means "to prostrate oneself" and in the opinion of most scholars means "to kiss."[3] This would imply deep adoration, reverence, and worship. Built into this understanding of prayer is a posture that conveys worshiping

God with deep awe. Sometimes we need postures that recover awe and reestablish that we have a God who is beyond our imaginings, the great I Am who delights in intimate communion. There are times when we need to fall down in prayer and other times when we need to lift our hands. What is important is that both the Old Testament and New Testament offer a model to include the body in a wide variety of postures. We must reclaim the rich heritage we have. The historic precedent does not suggest that these postures are mandatory, but that there is room for bringing our bodies to this sacred act of prayer, and as soon as we think we must use a certain posture to pray to God, or to win approval, we miss the entire point. Our postures and gestures are a gift to us so we can truly commune with God with all our heart, soul, and body. They are not a noose to wear around our neck as if we could only come to God if we kneel or raise our hands. The tragedy in the Church has been to communicate that only certain postures are appropriate and some are more appropriate than others. We are too complex as humans to be limited or confined to one posture, such as only kneeling or only raising hands. We need to have freedom to embody the wide range of postures found in Scripture, from rolling on the ground to dancing in ecstasy.

The New Testament also gives witness to dance being used as an expression of joy and thanksgiving. Since dance is marked by rejoicing in the Old Testament, it is only natural that this would overflow into New Testament times. We see this expressed in the story of the Prodigal Son coming home to his father. What happens when the wayward son returns? The father is filled with compassion and embraces him, welcoming him back home. This familiar passage in the Gospel of Luke (15:11–31) tells of the other son coming home and hearing the celebration, which is marked by music and dancing. Here we see the continued relationship between joy and dance. This was a time of celebration, and what better way to embody that celebration than to dance!

Dancing was a natural outpouring of how this culture expressed joy. To dance or not to dance is not a theological issue in the New Testament, where little attention is given to it, aside from a few citings of its presence.[4] Many scholars believe the lack of attention to dance in the New Testament suggests that the dance in New Testament times paralleled the presence of dance in the Jewish tradition, and there was no need to allude to it specifically.[5] People did not debate whether dance was an expression of God, because it was a natural part of life, just as music may be in the contemporary Church.

Our visual imaginations have seen so many pictures of Jesus in European attire, it is easy to think he might have actually been English, Dutch, or Italian. Most painters would paint Jesus in their particular cultural setting. These images, so marked by the era of the Renaissance, have indelibly been marked on our imaginations. Beautiful as they sometimes are, they do not give us a picture of a Jewish Jesus, one who was steeped in this gutsy, earthy culture that loved to express itself through the language of the body. Reminding ourselves of the particularities and flavor of this culture enables us to understand how the body was central to Jewish expression.

Life As Embodied Prayer

The New Testament gives us more than an example of postural prayer and dance; it shows a way of being embodied in the life of faith. We see, lived out most completely through Jesus, an embodied way of *being* in the world. As Jesus walked along this earth, he touched people as he healed them, gathered the children in his arms, kneeled to God in prayer, washed the disciples' feet with his hands, broke bread with them, and finally gave his body up on the cross. In his touching and healing, washing and gathering, kneeling and breaking, we partake of a continued bodily prayer, a prayer on behalf of those he cherished. We do not get a picture of a God who is distant, uninvolved, or so mystical as to be out of the body. Rather, Jesus gives us an image of a Creator who is deeply connected to the body, a God who is there *with* us. Attentive.

We usually know intuitively when someone is or is not attentive to us. I personally find it disconcerting when I am speaking to someone and he or she is looking all around, his or her body language suggesting that this person is really somewhere else. I feel minimized and am not apt to risk being vulnerable. The picture that I receive of Jesus is of someone with whom I can be totally vulnerable because he was present to life in both body and soul. Present to God. Present to us. Being present means being connected to our bodies, embracing our bodies, and letting our bodies become a reflection of what lies deeply inside us. Jesus' gestures and postures manifest the love of God, confirming we are the sons and daughters, friends and lovers, of God.

The Washing of Feet As Bodily Prayer

Jesus' act of washing the disciples' feet in and of itself is a bodily prayer. The account in the Gospel of John reveals Jesus as servant-Messiah and the disciples as the ones who will be marked by a servant heart. Jesus portrays this by initiating a gesture of tangible intimacy — the washing of feet. Jesus includes parts of the body we often render with ambivalence — our feet! Our feet take more abuse than we realize; rooting our bodies, they hold, sustain, and carry our frames through the space of our lives. Particularly in the culture of the New Testament times feet took abuse; exposed feet in well-worn sandals were continually bare to the dust of the earth, to roads that would be considered primitive by twentieth-century standards. Jesus' act was appropriate; however, he surprises the disciples not only by his action, but by doing it in the middle of the Passover meal, heightening its significance. The customary thing to do would be to wash people's feet as they entered from the outside, but Jesus takes an ordinary custom and pulls the sacredness out of it by changing its time and place and charging it with meaning.

People often think feet are an unbecoming part of the

body; their toes aren't even, corns may be sticking out, and of course there is that distinctive odor that can exude from the loveliest of people. That makes Jesus' act all the more profound — he ministered to the uncomely parts, the parts that we want to cover.

Footwashing was commonplace in New Testament times; in fact it was customary hospitality to provide water for a guest to wash his/her feet and an act of devotion for a disciple to wash his master's feet. Nonetheless, it was still a vulnerable bodily offering. Jesus took an ordinary custom and transformed it into a bodily prayer; one that not only includes our soul, but our bodies. This physical act of love extends from servant to master, master to servant, brother to brother, sister to sister, and friend to enemy. Body to body, flesh to flesh, hands to feet. Jesus' healing hands touch his followers bodies', and they are inwardly washed as well.

Washing feet takes risks, particularly within a worship service in the twentieth century; it is a physical act that steps over boundaries, ushering in a radical way of seeing one another. It is about seeing and bearing Christ in one another, tearing down the invisible walls of who has gained more insight on the spiritual journey. As we wash the feet of one another, we again wash Christ's feet, pouring oil on his head and entering a sacrament of bodily prayer.

Jesus could just have spoken his message — the words in and of themselves are strong, but the bodily gesture of gently taking a foot in his carpenter hands was a potent remembering of the heart of God. God continues to make known a love to us that goes beyond our limited understanding. As communities of faith we not only need to symbolically wash one another's feet, but to consider the richness of weaving this bodily ritual into our liturgies and worship. This could be a bodily prayer, a prayer of reminder that a suffering messiah is marked on our bodies, and a prayer to see one another with the eyes of Jesus. In this act we can again claim the heart of God through our bodies.

Not only did Jesus love us through his bodily acts of prayer, but he also received love through his own body. As he so readily washed the disciples' feet, he received the anointing of precious perfume on his feet by a woman who also wiped his feet with her tears. In this act of anointing recorded in all four gospels, the repeated element is that Jesus accepted her gift of bodily devotion.[6]

The ultimate prayer of Jesus was the prayer of brokenness, giving his life on the cross. Through the cross we enter into a complete act of surrender, a surrender that illuminates the love of God to us through a broken body. Life comes through brokenness, as love is met in brokenness.

Love is again met in the Resurrection and allows for the Spirit of God to dwell within our bodies. When Jesus left us, we were sent the Spirit to dwell in our hearts and bodies. It is the same Spirit who Paul so beautifully reminds us prays through us:

Likewise the Spirit helps us in our weakness; for we do not know how to pray as we ought, but that very Spirit intercedes with sighs too deep for words.

And God, who searches the heart, knows what is the mind of the Spirit, because the Spirit intercedes for the saints according to the will of God. (Rom 8:26–27)

Some of the sighs that the Spirit prays within us are sighs of movement, bodily sighs that go beyond our words. It would be more than presumptuous to think that Paul had in mind bodily prayer in this passage, yet I think there is an important application. No matter if we speak our prayers, dance our prayers, or simply fall to the ground, or reach our hands to the heavens, the Spirit within prays through us. I have often thought of this passage when I dance my prayers, knowing that though I may not even comprehend the meaning of my movements, God is familiar with the language of the Spirit praying in and through my body.

Even our literal sighs and breath can be prayers within themselves. Sometimes our sighs speak directly from our heart to God's heart. The words that cannot be formed are given over to our sighs. Not long ago, I was co-leading a workshop called "Music for the Paschal Season" with another leader, Kelly Walker. We both led the participants in a voice and body warm-up. As we began, he had us just sigh our prayers, from deep within our gut. Our breath and our sighs literally became our prayer. I found it a very profound experience to hear a congregation of sighs, bellowing out to God in prayer. I have often thought what a wonderful way to offer intercessory prayers on behalf of the suffering in our midst.

One aspect of prayer that the New Testament gives

us is intercessory prayer, praying on behalf of others. Corporately and privately the Church has had a long tradition of praying for others. Most often we have expressed these prayers verbally, beseeching God to do something on behalf of another — to give comfort, health, wisdom, and so on. Many of us have experienced what it is like to be carried by others' prayers. There are times when we cannot pray, though we are in such need, and we know it is only because others are praying on our behalf that we continue to experience grace in our lives.

I would like to expand the New Testament model of intercessory prayer to include the language of our bodies. Let me give an example of how this can be done. In one class I was teaching, I had my students break up into twos. Each was to share, if the student felt free to do so, a need s/he would like offered in prayer. If someone did not feel comfortable sharing with the partner, s/he could refrain. The person who was praying for the need would translate the verbal prayer into movement, gathering the cries and whispers of his/her heart and giving them to God. It could be as simple as a gathering motion of the hands, lifting them in the air over the partner. Or it could take the nature of expressing the person's particular need in creative movement and letting it go to God.

One student, whom I will call Dorothy, found this exercise particularly meaningful. As she expressed through her limbs her prayer for her partner, whom I will call Ruth, she experienced God's deep compassion for Ruth. At first Dorothy felt a bit vulnerable and unsafe doing this exercise. After all it is not every day you pray over a person with movement. But as she allowed herself to enter this process, she had a deep sense that God was with her and, because God was there, it was safe. In her own assurance of acceptance and safety with God, she knew it was safe for both her and Ruth to move in God's presence. Dorothy initially found this exercise very risky because she did not have anything preconceived in her mind about how to pray through her body for her partner. In the midst of doing the exercise she began to have the sense that the Spirit flowed and prayed through her body on behalf of Ruth. In turn, Ruth was able to sense God's compassion through Dorothy's movements over her. At one point Dorothy held Ruth while she was sitting down and gently rocked her. In this tender moment we see the body of Christ, truly carrying one another's burdens.

As we pray on behalf of others through our bodies, we give ourselves the opportunity to truly "enter" their pain. When we express in movement the pain of loneliness, anger, rejection, or disappointment, we may see a particular need in a more accurate light. God walks with us; we must walk with others. We need pragmatic ways to truly walk in another's shoes.

The Place of Solitude

Jesus gives us a model for praying in solitude, which is the geography conducive for engaging in bodily prayer. Jesus went apart to places away from the hustle and bustle to meet God in the wilderness. Solitude is the soil that prayer must be nourished in. As Henri Nouwen has so aptly said, "Solitude is the place of mourning and the place of dancing."[7] Solitude grooms us for hearing the laments in our hearts and dances in our souls. Eventually all other concerns dissipate, and we are left alone to present to ourselves and be present to God.

Our bodies are a vulnerable and precious place, and many of us may feel too exposed to bring our bodies to prayer and risk being interrupted by a friend, roommate, or spouse. It is crucial to have a place where we feel safe. Safe to be naked with our feelings, thoughts, groans, and cries. A place where the tears can come. A place where we can listen. Jesus beckons us to pray by going into our room, closing the door, and praying to God, who is unseen (Mt 6:6). Prayer requires that we have the nourishment of solitude. Verbal, reflective, or meditative prayer can be done while riding on a bus, subway, or in a car, but it is not as easy to pray with our bodies in a public place. We need to find a private place, the place where we can meet the Beloved with all of who we are.

The Prayer of Attentiveness

One of the most common postures of prayer in the New Testament is the posture of standing. In fact, it has been said that "few customs are more frequently mentioned by early Christian writers than the practice of praying in the standing posture."[8] Through Jesus' words we see the pattern of standing: "Whenever you *stand* praying forgive, if you have anything against anyone; so that your Father in heaven may also forgive you your trespasses" (Mk 11:25). Standing was assumed when in prayer. This is further developed in postures of worship. The book of Revelation continues this posture as we see the worshipers "standing before the throne and before the Lamb" (Rev 7:9). Standing demonstrates attentiveness to God.

Many churches today still stand during the whole service, as the Eastern Orthodox Church does. In other denominations standing is done throughout the liturgy at specific times to worship, pray, hear the gospel, or proclaim afresh as a community our faith in God. Few of us stand in private prayer at home, but I would like for us to reconsider the importance of this posture, which is so integral to our daily lives. Some of us cannot think of "standing" in prayer when we have vocations that literally call us to stand throughout the day. We need to sit down.

But many times throughout our day we find ourselves standing in some kind of neutral position. Maybe we are waiting for a bus, doing the dishes, standing and waiting at someone's desk, waiting in line at the bank or grocery store, or standing and taking in the beauty of creation. This posture can be a pragmatic reminder to us that we are called to be "attentive." Attentive to the whispers of God. We can engage in, as Brother Lawrence calls it, "practicing the presence of God," through the posture of standing. As we stand, we can remember through our bodies to offer our moments to God, as mundane as they can be. Paul sums this up in the first book of Corinthians when he says, "Keep *alert, stand* firm in your faith, be courageous, be strong. Let all that you do be done in love" (1 Cor 16:13). As we are metaphorically standing firm in our faith, we may be reminded in the ordinary posture of standing to be attentive to the presence of God, and of God's attentiveness to us.

The New Testament offers us a wonderful tradition of bodily prayer, but more than that it offers us an embodied way of being, through the example of Jesus. We are encouraged to be attentive to life in all of its groans, bursts, pains, and joys. We are asked to be physically and spiritually present — to receive fully and give fully. In the beautiful example of Jesus may we be given food for the journey of intertwining the spiritual-physical life of prayer.

Notes

1. See 1 Timothy 2:8 and Ephesians 3:14, Acts 21:5.
2. See Luke 22:41 and Matthew 26:39.
3. For a thorough explanation of the word *proskyneo* used in the New Testament see "Proskyneo" by H. Schonweiss and C. Brown in Colin Brown, ed., *The New International Dictionary of New Testament Theology*, Vol. 2 (Grand Rapids, Mich.: Zondervan Publishing House, 1967), pp. 875–79.
4. See Matthew 11:16–17 and Luke 7:31–33, 15:25.
5. See Ronald Gagne in Ronald Gagne, Thomas Kane, and Robert VerEecke, eds., *Introducing Dance in Christian Worship* (Washington, D.C.: Pastoral Press, 1984), p. 35.
6. See John 12:1–8, Matthew 26:6–13, Mark 14:3–9, Luke 7:37–39.
7. H. Nouwen in a talk in Burnaby, British Columbia, April 8, 1994.
8. V. Staley quoted in Markus Bockmuehl, "Should We Kneel to Pray?" in *Crux*, Vol. XXVl, No. 3 (Sept. 1990).

Chapter 7

A TAPESTRY OF MOVEMENT

Ritual in the Church

⎯⎯⎯⎯⎯⎯⎯⎯ ℘ ⎯⎯⎯⎯⎯⎯⎯⎯

A look at the Church at large, through a wide-angle lens, would reveal a spectacular tapestry of bodily ritual in prayer, worship, and proclamation. In some churches there is kneeling or bowing, in others there is lifting of hands, in some there is processional movement, and in some we see spontaneous dance or choreographed dance. Postures can be as ordinary as exchanging a hand for the greeting of peace or making a sign of the cross, or they can be more elaborate, as in a set-gesture prayer to the Lord's Prayer. Unfortunately many of the Church traditions that encourage lifting of the hands may not encourage kneeling and vice versa. This can be discouraging, for we yearn for the full gamut of bodily expression, bending and lifting, dancing and lamenting.

The use of bodily gesture, movement, and dance is not something new to the Church or some innovative idea to make the Church more contemporary. Church history provides a rich and comprehensive legacy of dance, movement, bodily gestures, and postures since the first few centuries of the early Church to the present day. There has certainly been an ebb and flow of the presence of movement in the Church, but it has always been evident in some form. To appreciate where we are going, it is important to have a sense of the past. This book cannot afford the space to treat the rich historical legacy in depth. There are, however, some fine resources, particularly in the area of the history of dance and Christianity, that provide a good historical overview.[1]

This chapter will highlight some of the movement ritual of the past, in order to bring a sense of continuity to movement in the Church. Carolyn Deitering, liturgist, dancer, and author, has said so aptly:

> True ritual is *living* ritual, containing the past, embracing the present, and allowing the future to unfold. Ritual which does not grow, naturally and organically, with the faith of the people who practice it, loses it claim to be ritual.[2]

As we bring bodily movement to the life of the Church, we include the gestures of the past and introduce the gestures of the present: The time-honored lifting of our hands to take the Eucharist can be as meaningful as doing an original pew dance. Each gesture is an affirmation that we are an incarnated people; God comes to us through flesh and blood in the Incarnation, and we reach with our hands for the bread and wine as an act of faith. Every movement within the liturgy, whether small or large, is an embodied prayer. We cannot sit or stand, talk or sing, without some form of movement.

Some of us may have engaged in different postures or gestures in church that have become rote. Kneeling or raising hands may be so usual and expected that we need to find a new way of experiencing these movements. I have found that as I introduce a wider movement vocabulary during workshops to churches, the movements that congregations have had all along become more meaningful. When there is opportunity to experience more of our bodies, we begin to truly feel the weightedness of our knees when we kneel, or the freedom of lifting our hands with open palms. The kneeling in and of itself is a prayer, and the raising of hands is a prayer. Our bodies become alive, and our very cells want to leap out of the pew.

Our postures and gestures truly reflect what is going on inside us — they are expressive of our proclamation of faith. I have introduced simple movement to the Lord's Prayer to many congregations from diverse denominations and find that this prayer has become more significant to people once they have had the opportunity to enter it with their whole bodies. They already know it so well verbally, it is easy to bring gestures and postures to the words. I now find it difficult to pray the Lord's Prayer without my body; it somehow seems incomplete. As Doug Adams has said, "...for people to pray, "Your kingdom come" while in a sedentary posture is to suggest that they can do little about it, whereas if they stood with arms raised and extended forward, the postures would declare that they can and will be agents of its advent."[3]

When we bring our bodies to the prayers of history, we pray "actively." It is not as if we are not praying actively when we just verbalize prayers, but there are times when our bodies need to awaken us to the words again so we can experience them anew.

Movement can startle us out of complacency. As with any art form, it can make what we've heard all along ring in our hearts with truth. Truth bears renewed witness in our bodies as we make the sign of the cross, release our hands in praise, or fold our hands to pray. Our postures can reveal our hearts, and our hearts can reveal our postures. Our bodies become a visible sign of inner grace. Spirit becomes matter, and matter becomes spirit. I often think of the example of the Armenian liturgy. At the "inclination," when the people bow down in adoration, the priest is directed to pray that the Holy Spirit might "keep them entire and stamp upon their hearts the posture of their bodies."[4]

Let us turn now to some of the ways the Church has used movement, gestures, postures, and dance in ritual throughout the ages. It is no secret that the Church has clearly had a love-hate relationship with the body since the time of Christ. There are times when movement was embraced and times when it was frowned upon. This is due to various reasons: changes in philosophical or theological ideas about the body, associations of dance with mystery cults or pagan religions, changes in Church leadership, and Reformation history. The list could go on.[5] Debate has not been a stranger to the Church and certainly wasn't a stranger to Jesus. In the midst of continued disagreements we still see today many congregations all over the world being a "dancing Church," modeling the integration of various postures, gestures, and dance into the life of worship.[6]

The Early Church

The early Church, which incorporates the first four centuries A.D., has numerous references to dance and movement as part of worship. At points dance is symbolically associated with "heavenly bliss" or the "angels dancing"; dance is symbolic of the spiritual movement of the inner life. At other points there are references to actual dancing. Following are some of the Church Fathers' thoughts on dance, which give an idea of its function in the early Church.

Clement of Alexandria (150–216 A.D.), in a sermon, refers to "the daughters of God, the fair lambs, who celebrate the holy rites of the Word, raising a sober choral dance."[7] Gregory the Wonder Worker (213–270 A.D.) speaks of dance in connection with the martyrs, as it was customary to do dances at the martyrs' tombs. He says, "By what acts of grace can we return the love which he bore for God? If you do wish, then let us in his honor perform our customary dances."[8] Ambrose (340–397 A.D.), who was bishop of Milan, requested that persons about to be baptized approach the font dancing and defines dance as "spiritual applause."[9] Even the well-known Augustine (354–430 A.D.) regarded dance as bringing one's bodily members in accord with the love of God.[10]

These are only a few examples of movement and dance in the early Church. The form of dance was simple, often consisting of ring or circle dances, and the emphasis was on its symbolic significance. Gesture was integral to the early Church, and one can visually see this through the iconography as well as the catacomb paintings of the early Church. The "orante figure," for instance, seen painted in the catacombs, depicts someone standing in a posture with hands raised to the chest and palms facing outward. This has become a familiar posture of prayer, painted into history.[11]

The gesture of making the sign of the cross originated early and is still an example of writing the Incarnation on one's body.

As said by Tertullian many centuries ago:

At every forward step and movement, at every going in and out, when we put on our clothes and shoes, when we bathe, when we sit at table, when we light the lamps, on couch, on seat, in all the ordinary actions of everyday life, we trace upon the forehead the sign of the cross.[12]

The sign of the cross is an embodied prayer that the Church has had for centuries, and today is most visible in Catholic and Orthodox churches. The Eastern Orthodox Church has developed its interpretation. The thumb and the first two fingers are joined to symbolize the Trinity. The third and little fingers are bent and pressed together into the palm to signify the One Person of Christ in two natures. Touching the forehead is a profession of faith in God who is over all; moving down to the breast confesses Christ who came to us bringing salvation; and passing the hand from shoulder to shoulder honors the Holy Spirit who is the bond of love between God and Son.[13] In this small gesture there is packed volumes of theology.

The Medieval Church

The early Church became the Medieval Church (400–1400 A.D.), and in a variety of ways movement was continued within the Church, particularly as it grew in Western Europe. Dance was used at different feast days: the deacons' festival dance on St. Stephen's Day, the priests' festival dance on St. John's Day, the subdeacons' festival dance on the Feast of Epiphany, and the choirboys' dance on Holy Innocents' Day. As well, the children's festival included dancing at the divine service. In the seventh century the archbishop Isidore of Seville even composed a ritual of choreography that is still celebrated three times a year in the Cathedral of Seville. And of course by 1100 A.D. the well-known "Mystery Plays" came into the liturgy, where the gospel message was incorporated into theatrical events. The form of the theatrical play, as we now know it, basically came out of these Mystery Plays. The labyrinth dance was done annually on Easter Sunday, and during the later Middle Ages it was danced to a three-step rhythm to the accompaniment of the Easter antiphon. It was danced by the dean and other canons in the floor of the nave near the west door of the cathedral. What a wonderful way to use sacred space! There are so many parts of a church that can be used to incorporate movement. We often think of only certain parts of the sanctuary, but from the point of view of a dancer there are the aisles, the entrance, the corners, and the platform or altar. One can only imagine all the diverse ways a congregation could let their bodies give voice throughout the magnificent architecture of a cathedral.

One of the simple dances present within the Medieval Church, and easy to incorporate in worship today, is the Tripudium. The Tripudium is a dance consisting of three steps forward and one step back. This is symbolic of the nature of the Christian life; every time we take a few steps forward, we take one step back. I have taught many people these simple movements to familiar hymns or choruses. In this way we establish continuity with those who have danced their faith before us.

A beautiful citing of movement in the Medieval Church is in some of the writings of the monastic orders. The Franciscans were noted as "singing servants of Christ." As so well said by Fra Jacapone da Todi, a Franciscan in the thirteenth century, "Oh, that each one who loves the Lord would join in the dance, singing of his devotion."[14] In an account of Saint Francis and his eleven followers, we learn that when granted permission to establish the order of Franciscans, they could not contain their joy and danced in front of Pope Innocent III.[15]

The Renaissance Church

In the Renaissance there was a burst of creative energy, as humanity experienced a flowering in both the arts and sciences. Artists like Michelangelo, da Vinci, Raphael, and Brunelleschi changed the scope of art in the Western world as they sought to bring perspective to the visual arts. The world of classical ballet also came to prominence in the fifteenth and sixteenth centuries, further reflecting this flowering of the arts. Movement in the Church continued to be evident during the period of the Renaissance, particularly in processions. Artists such as Botticelli and Donatello give us a glimpse of the spiritual nature of dance through their depiction of angels doing a ring dance in heaven.

Visual art within the Church was extremely prominent, and in fact the Church became a generous patron of the arts. We now have museums that are full of works by well-known painters, thanks to the Church. Unfortunately, in some corners, emphasis shifted from the arts as an expression of worship to an object of worship. The use of relics and indulgences is an example of this shift; thus the image of Christ became elevated above Christ himself. The Reformers of the sixteenth century such as Martin Luther, Huldrych Zwingli, and John Calvin stressed that we are "saved by grace, and not by works" and began to restore worship to its essentials. During the Reformation art was taken from many churches, even destroyed. Tragically the attitude toward the arts within the Church greatly suffered, particularly within the Protestant limb of the Church.[16] The presence of dance in worship was also to suffer greatly, and by the Post-Renaissance Period (1700–1900) dance was hardly visible in Protestant or Catholic churches.[17] Religious expression of dance survived only in isolated pockets.

Post-Renaissance

One of the pockets where movement and gesture were visible was within the Shakers. The Shakers were a religious community founded in 1747 in England who came to the Eastern United States in 1774. The actual term *Shaker* comes from the rapid up-and-down movement of the hands, with the action mostly in the wrists. The Shakers have a fascinating history of using gestures of the hands and feet, to which they gave profound meanings. The palms facing upward were equated with receiving God's blessing. The quick up-and-down shaking movement expressed the open petition "Come, Life Eternal." Even turning was symbolic: As the Shakers turned away from evil and around toward good, one would hear them saying, "I'll turn, turn, turn, turn away from all evil, And come, come, come, come into the gospel."[18]

The symbolic actions of the Shakers were further lived out in their dances. The "Heavenly March" introduced by Lucy Wright in the early nineteenth century was symbolic of marching the heavenly road and walking the streets of the New Jerusalem. The circle dance "Wheel-Within-a-Wheel" was done in three concentric circles, a metaphor of the all-inclusiveness of the gospel.

The Shakers' contribution to bodily prayer and sacred

dance is notable. As articulated so well by one of their leaders:

> Prayer is the sincere desire and breathing of the soul; therefore, we seldom pray vocally; as God knows the language, and desires of our hearts, a composition of words, expressive thereof, is, to him (who knows best what we stand in need of), not necessary.[19]

The Shakers had a beautiful understanding of prayer being the "breathing of the soul," and a genuine sense of God hearing and seeing the gestures of their hearts. Some liturgists have been inspired to incorporate some of the Shakers' services in the Church today and seen worship greatly enriched.[20]

The Influence of Modern Dance

A significant element in the history of dance that influenced the expressive use of movement in religious expression was the rise of modern dance in the twentieth century. Modern dancers, notably Ted Shawn and Ruth St. Denis, sought to bring the sacred dimension to their art. As said by St. Denis:

> Dance should lead all the arts because it is a great sacramental of harmonious living — an outward and visible sign of an inward and spiritual grace.[21]

Ted Shawn echoes St. Denis's statement in saying,

> And the greatest constant of all is that here in the
> dance we experience a rhythmic beauty, the activity
> of God Himself.[22]

The vocabulary of dance changed as the great pioneers, like Martha Graham, Doris Humphrey, Isadora
Duncan, and José Limón, stretched the bounds of what
had been considered dance. A variety of movement techniques emerged, from the "contractions" of Graham to
the "fall and recovery" technique of Humphrey. The
range and scope of dance was broadened, paving the
way for interpretive movement to be integrated into the
Church, using both professional techniques and impro-
visations by lay people.

Our Need for Ritual

Since then, the tapestry of movement has greatly in-
creased in the Church. This is now well documented,
and I would refer you to the resources in the back of
this book to see the beautiful and diverse ways dance is
used in the Church. The important principle, however, is
not how fancy, complex, or sophisticated movement can
be within the Church, and there is a place for both pol-
ished and more ordinary movement. There will always
be a wide scope of expression, as well as levels of quality
in movement, just as there is in musical expression. Each
church will have different resources available to it; a little

country church may not, for instance, have the cultural resources available to a big-city church.

What is important is that there is permission to bring our bodies to the dimension of worship and prayer within the life of the Church. It is also critical that there be consistency, just as there is in other parts of religious expression. It is part of the nature of ritual to be repeated over and over again, drawing us like breath, to come to God. Movement as well must be repeated in order to become part of us. When we learn to walk, we must continue to keep walking; so in bodily ritual, we must have the opportunity to do it over and over again in order for it to become a part of us. In turn, the Spirit ignites ritual to make it enliven our hearts and bodies.

It is my belief that worship is not something just done in church, but it is integral to every part of life. Movement ritual nourishes our faith and can take place in the privacy of our home or in the openness of creation. We can incorporate ritual within the daily parts of our lives, from a bodily prayer in the morning to invite God into our day to a specific time of devotion during our perhaps hectic schedule. In this way we bring the history of ritualized movement to our very doors, knowing that all along the Church has been an embodied people. We just need to proclaim it again through our bodies.

Notes

1. See E. Louis Backman, *Religious Dances in the Christian Church and in Popular Medicine* (London: George Allen & Unwin, Ltd., 1952); J. G. Davies, *Liturgical Dance: An Historical,*

Theological and Practical Handbook (London: SCM Press, 1984); Ronald Gagne, Thomas Kane, and Robert VerEecke, *Introducing Dance in Christian Worship* (Washington, D.C.: The Pastoral Press, 1984); and Margaret Fisk Taylor, *A Time to Dance: Symbolic Movement in Worship* (Austin, Tex.: The Sharing Company, 1967, rev. 1981).

2. Carolyn Deitering, *The Liturgy as Dance and the Liturgical Dancer* (New York: Crossroad, 1984).

3. Doug Adams, "Vitalizing Worship in Dance" (reprint from "Military Chaplains' Review," Spring 1979), p. 2.

4. See Davies, p. 162.

5. For a good and concise treatment of the history of dance/movement in the Church see Ronald Gagne, Ch. 3, "Cultic Movement in Liturgical Prayer from the Fourth Century to the Present," in Ronald Gagne, Thomas Kane, and Robert VerEecke, *Introducing Dance in Christian Worship* (Washington, D.C.: The Pastoral Press, 1984), pp. 45–90.

6. Such international organizations as the Sacred Dance Guild and International Christian Dance Fellowship are a testimony to the many ways movement is being used in the Church around the world.

7. Clement of Alexandria, "Exhortation to the Heathen" in *Ante-Nicene Fathers,* Vol. II (New York: Charles Scribner's Sons, 1899), p. 205.

8. Quoted in Davies, p. 43.

9. Ambrose, "On Repentance," Vol. 2, Ch. 6, in Gagne, p. 48.

10. Augustine, "Sermon 311 6" (In *Natali Cypriani*) in Daniel A. Kister, "Dance and Theater in Christian Worship." *Worship,* Vol. 45 (Dec. 1971), p. 591.

11. For a good treatment of the importance of imagery in the early Church, see Margaret R. Miles, *Image as Insight: Visual Understanding in Western Christianity and Secular Culture* (Boston, Mass.: Beacon Press, 1985).

12. Tertullian, quoted in Davies, p. 160.

13. See Davies, p. 160.

14. Jacopone da Todi, in Renee Foatelli, *Les Danses Re-*

ligieuses dans le Christianisme (Paris, France: Editions Spes, 1947), p. 95.

15. See Walter Sorell, *Dance in Its Time* (New York: Columbia University Press, 1986), p. 11.

16. It is important to note that there were positive influences of the Reformation on art, for example, many of the Bibles were now illustrated and put into English, as well as content of art changing from merely religious works to content of everyday experiences.

17. See Ronald Gagne, in Gagne, Kane, VerEecke, p. 59.

18. Quoted in Margaret Fisk Taylor, *A Time to Dance: Symbolic Movement in Worship* (Austin, Tex.: The Sharing Company, rev. 1981), p. 124.

19. Quoted in Marjorie Procter-Smith, *Women in Shaker Community and Worship* (Queenston, Ontario: Edwin Mellen Press, 1985), p. 161.

20. See J. G. Davies, P. van Zyl, and F. M. Young, *A Shaker Dance Service Reconstructed* (Birmingham, England: Institute for the Study of Worship and Religious Architecture, University of Birmingham, 1984).

21. Denis, quoted in Davies, p. 5.

22. Ted Shawn quoted in Jean Morrison Brown, ed., *The Vision of Modern Dance* (Princeton, N.J.: Princeton Book Company, Publishers, 1979), p. 32.

Chapter 8

THE PSALMS

A Movement Map to the Heart

❧

The psalms capture our hearts with total immediacy. The words do not slide across the skin but penetrate to marrow and bone. The author of Hebrews tells us that the word of God has the capacity to penetrate to the joints and marrow of our lives (Heb 4:12); with rich, clear-cut imagery these verses slash away any pretense.

Our emotions cannot hide when the psalms grip us. The psalms explore the emotional terrain of pain, joy, turmoil, hope, doubt, anger, or feelings of abandonment by God. The psalms encourage us to give ourselves permission "to be" and "to live" in the emotional terrain of our own lives. We are invited to see even experiences such as doubt, or fear, as having something valuable to teach us on our journey. As John Calvin said, the psalms are an "anatomy to all the parts of the soul." They uncover the skeletons hidden in our body-soul and give us fuel for the road of transformation. Often the flow of life dictates that we persevere, while many attitudes and emotions are buried within the surface of our exterior lives. Our bodies become a reminder to our hearts, giving us warning signals of what is spiritually and emotionally needing our attention. When our hearts betray us, our bodies ring true. The psalms ring true to every part of us.

Richard was an engineer who came to study at a theological college. He had been competent professionally and esteemed as a leader in his church. In his quest to discover the creative side of himself he took a class with me on the arts. We were doing a section on movement, and I had students do a simple exercise inspired by Psalm 19 and Psalm 150. Psalm 19 so eloquently outlines the beauty of Creation, and Psalm 150 speaks of everything praising God. Each person in the class was to put a simple movement to something that may have inspired him/her from Creation; anything from the wind in the trees to human emotions, from funny to serious. We each took a turn sharing our small movement phrase and then taught the class our individual movement. As Richard came to share his piece, tears rolled from his eyes. They were not tears of sadness, but tears of joy and relief. For Richard to be able to include his body in expression was an extremely freeing act. The class had the privilege to share in this moment of his journey, in the recovery of his body. The body was something that he had been encouraged to ignore and gloss over. Subsequent to this time of celebrating his bodily nature, Richard had an outpouring of creativity and growth in his life. It was one more step in God's pull toward transformation and wholeness.

God calls us to wholeness, and nowhere do we see this unity more deeply than in the poetry of the Bible. The psalmist says there is no soundness in his body as a result of his sin (Ps 38:3) or that his heart is glad and his tongue rejoices and his body also will rest secure (Ps 16:9). The psalmist also exclaims, "My whole being will claim, who is like you O Lord?" (Ps 35:10). The Hebrew for *whole* is *esem,* which literally translated is *bones.* The verse could be rendered, "All my bones will claim, Who is like you, O Lord?" Body and soul, heart and mind, find a physical voice in the cries of the people of God through the psalms.

The Israelites' hope is found in the midst of their cries, laments, and heartrending dialogue with their Maker. The people become utterly vulnerable, naked before the Holy One, waiting and sometimes demanding to be transformed.

We, too, can become naked before God in our journey through the psalms. We do not have to put on an act that everything is all right, that we are always the triumphant Christians. No! We come in brokenness; God desires to be given a broken spirit, not sacrifice (Ps 51). The psalms invite us to be broken, molded, and transformed in the fire of the Spirit.

How can we discover the physicality of the psalms? How do we pray them into the depths of our souls, flesh, and fingertips? The Church has had a long tradition of praying and singing the psalms, allowing them to penetrate over and over until they become as breath. They are drawn in and out, as breath does blood, oxygenating our innermost hearts.

Many of us have memorized various psalms and have experienced their comfort in time of need. The rich tradition of *lectio divina* has given the Church a discipline to slowly pray the psalms, allowing them to settle into the heart.[1] My invitation to you is to have the psalms written on your bodies in the hope that they may become engraved on your bones.

By including the language of movement in praying or reciting the psalms, we allow God's word to take on a deeper dimension in our lives. As we begin to express the words and nuances of the psalms with our hands, feet, and torsos, its powerful metaphors sink into our spirits. Inner barriers are broken down, and we can truly pray the range of the psalmist's prayer from lament to joy. The poetry of the psalms becomes a spiritual map for the pilgrim, and gives a concrete guide for exploring the physicality of our spiritual life.

The Psalms in Personal Bodily Prayer

The psalms are one of the best places to start experimenting in bodily prayer because they cover the whole gamut of human experience: penitence, thanksgiving, doubt, despair, anger, joy, dialogue with God, hunger and sickness, adoration and worship. Fertile in visual metaphor, in the language of poets, they speak strikingly to the heart, creating lasting images. These images are easily translated into movement metaphors. Many psalms have verbs that are "movement verbs."[2] These are verbs that describe some kind of moving action, e.g., falling, sinking, stumbling, bowing, walking, standing, rising, skipping, dancing. These organic movements can be enlarged, diminished, and improvised in the process of exploring different ways of moving, for instance when creating in the choreographic process. Inherent in all principles of creative movement and dance, they are, however, actions that we all can do, not just dancers with years and years of training. These actions, which are basically pedestrian descriptions of everyday movements, take on a larger meaning as the psalmist parallels them to a place of spiritual formation.

> I will exalt you, O Lord,
> for you *lifted* me out of the depths
> and did not let my enemies gloat over me.
> O Lord my God, I called to you for help and you
>   healed me.
> O Lord, you *brought me up* from the grave;
> you spared me from *going down* into the pit.
>
> You *turned* my wailing into *dancing;*
> you removed my sackcloth and clothed me with joy
> that my heart may sing to you and not be silent.
> O Lord my God, I will give you thanks forever.
>
> (Psalm 30:1–3, 11–12, NIV)

One of the most familiar psalms of the psalter, Psalm 23, gives us a verse that many have carved on their heart: "Even though I *walk* through the valley of the shadow of death...." Walk is the central action to describe moving through a place of darkness. We walk

every day, sometimes to what we believe to be the shadow
of death, but how often do we think we can pray and
walk? The rhythm of our walk can be the rhythm of our
prayer; the very act of walking often allows me to physically and emotionally prepare to center on God. Many
times I want to pray, but my mind is cluttered with so
many details it is hard to relax and commune with God.
My body also wants physical attention, feeling sedentary
and needing to breathe in its own rhythm. There is a
small lake I often go to and walk around several times,
enjoying the wind in my face and the time to catch my
breath and listen to its rhythm. The act of walking allows
me to breathe out my distractions and be with God; each
step becomes a prayer in and of itself.

The psalmist describes intimacy and closeness with
God as having feet firmly put on the ground, or as having feet like the deer.[3] These metaphors of the body
describe another reality — an inner soulscape. And men
and women in despair use verbs like *sink* or *losing one's
foothold*.[4] The act of slipping is used as a parallel to
inward discouragement.[5]

We have learned to skip over the physical meaning
of these "movement words" and cerebrally take the sec-
ondary meaning, but as we've done so, the meaning has
weakened. What does it mean to feel as if your body is
sinking to the ground? What are you communicating?
What are you expressing when you feel as if your feet
are like those of a deer or when they feel firmly aligned
on level ground, no cliffs in sight? These are all creative-
movement words that can be readily improvised in order
to discover a more complete way of "hiding the word in

your body." Our body prayer can be as simple as sinking and rising. Sinking in our woundedness, in our sin, in our hurts, and rising to God in healing. We can sink and rise in many ways, in many moods, and in many motions: on the ground, with big movements or little movements, repetitive or quiet, rapidly or with pauses, to jazz or classical music, to drumbeats, or to only the quiet presence of the Beloved.

I often use the psalms as an exercise in embodied prayer in classes and workshops. Taking a few lines from a psalm and expressing it in movement can be a profound experience for some. People learn to pray from the inside out, and the psalm makes its home in the body. A few years ago, when I was teaching a "Dance and Theology" class, I had my students break up into groups and interpret Psalm 51 through creative movement. Most students in the class had minimal or no formal dance technique in their backgrounds, but wanted to explore the relationship between dance and faith. Some interpreted the verse alone, others worked in groups of two or three. I was struck by the power of each verse as it was interpreted — each person's own movement communicating the backbone of the verse. It was as if the cry for God's forgiveness could now be seen in a concrete way. No longer was it just a mental exercise, for as students interpreted this psalm of confession through their bodies, they met the words of God face-to-face, muscle-to-muscle, bone-to-bone. As the class shared their verses with one another, we were able to enter the confession of David in a new way. So when David cries out in this psalm for God to let his crushed bones rejoice, we could not only mentally, but also physically, enter into this tangible cry. In entering David's confession with interpretive movement, we were nudged to enter our own hard places and find forgiveness and rest. I later invited the class to dance Psalm 51 in a chapel service so the entire student body could communally enter confession in a physical manner.

As we interpret the psalms in movement, we allow them to be heard in a larger way, for our bodies remind us of their piercing truth. One of my favorite dances that I have choreographed is to Psalm 139. I usually dance this psalm and speak it at the same time, often with a musician improvising an instrumental accompaniment. I had always loved that psalm with its beautiful metaphors of being woven in the womb and its focus on God as intimate Creator. In the process of my choreographing and dancing this psalm, it has become a living extension of me. Every time I pray Psalm 139 in dance, it descends closer to my heart, and I am reminded of God's intricate love for me. I had exegeted,[6] studied, and prayed through Psalm 139 prior to dancing it. All of these were vitally important steps in leading me toward understanding; however, in allowing the words to be fleshed out by my muscles and ligaments, the visual metaphors of Psalm 139 were opened up to me in a new way. I have memorized it in my body, and it is eternally baked on my being.

It doesn't take a skilled performer to pray the psalms through the body. We all can move, even if our movement is restricted to certain parts of our bodies because of physical limitations. Movement is a God-given form of communication that we can all access. Many times I have seen men and women who have never danced or felt comfortable with their bodies bringing the psalmist's words to life as they incorporated their bodies in prayer. If they decide to share their interpretation or prayer with the rest of the class, the group is often profoundly moved and left with a lasting impression of the psalm.

The psalms are filled with images of movement and are not meant to remain static within our minds. They move, shake, alarm, and startle us to meet the God of the psalms from our very bones. They give a lifetime of resources to pray with the body.

The Psalms in Communal Bodily Prayer

You may feel comfortable to pray the psalms with your body in your own prayer closet. Actually the prayer closet has to be enlarged so you can move! However, we may feel quite inhibited to do this in congregational worship. What is appropriate in our individual devotion to God may not be suitable for the larger context of worship, but the question must be asked, How can I take what is meaningful to me in private devotion and integrate it in the larger faith community? How can my prayer extend to my body in the corporate life of the church, or is this something only for my personal conversation with God? The beauty of the psalms is that there is a history of utilizing them in song, Scripture readings, responsorial readings, choirs, and dance. They lend themselves to a wide form of interpretation.[7] Just as there are a variety of ways in which the psalms can be utilized in worship, there is also variety in the way we may incorporate our bodies. Whatever the Church can do with the art form of music can also be done with the art form of movement and dance. As the Church can be prepared for meeting God through a soloist singing a psalm, it can also prepare for meeting God in worship through a soloist or group interpreting the psalm in dance. Even though the worshiper may be sitting in a pew or chair, he or she can kinesthetically be taken through the psalmist's words as the dancer's limbs extend the meaning in her/his body. The congregation can physically and spiritually be drawn into God's presence as the word of God is incarnated in dance.

For centuries the psalms have been sung and put to music. The psalter has been called the songbook of the Old Testament. Movements and dance accompanying the psalms have been a historical tradition throughout the history in Jewish and Christian faith.

Simple movements and dances can be put to a few lines of a psalm or a complete psalm, and congregations can enter in jubilantly celebrating an incarnational faith. Psalms 149 and 150 boldly beckon the believer to praise God with all his/her breath incorporating string, noise, harp, body, and soul to the living God.

The fixed space of the church will also determine the kind of movement that can be incorporated in praying and singing the psalms corporately. Every space has limitations and advantages. I have seen movement incorporated into the tiniest of spaces, including crowded pews, small platforms, and altars, with a mass of wired technology cluttering every inch of free space. The simple movement of swaying back and forth holding one another's hands in the body of Christ can be a physical way of praying the psalmist's words. Any gathering can utilize simple circle dances to the psalmist's words.

One of the most accessible ways of incorporating the psalms in corporate prayer is in responsorial reading. This tradition is woven in diverse denominations and styles of worship. Reading the psalms corporately lets them ring loudly through our bodies. The congregation may repeat one line in between the verses as in Psalm 136, which is especially written for a response. The words "God's love endures forever"[8] are interfaced between each verse. The congregation could be led in simple gestures to these few words by a worship leader, pastor, or member of the congregation. As the gestures are repeated over and over again, they become as familiar as brushing one's teeth. We begin to take our bodies as well as our hearts and minds to church. To gaze out and see the congregation extending their bodies together in unison as a corporate prayer is for me a glimpse of the kingdom of God. We not only pray to God with our lips and hearts, but we also rise in one complete motion echoing the cries and whispers of our bodies' longings. Following the historical tradition of corporately praying the psalms, we move to the rhythm of the One who gave the inspiration of the psalms.

Notes

1. *Lectio Divina,* or divine reading, is the discipline originating from the fifteen-hundred-year-old tradition of monastic prayer; a discipline of slowly reading the psalms in a meditative, prayerful way. For contemporary guides to praying through the psalms see Eugene Peterson, *Answering God: The Psalms As Tools for Prayer* (San Francisco, Calif.: Harper & Row, 1989) and Donald E. Collins, *Like Trees That Grow Beside a Stream: Praying Through the Psalms* (Nashville, Tenn.: Upper Room Books, 1991).

2. *Movement verbs* is a term phrased by this author; however, I am indebted to the pioneers in the field of dance education, particularly Rudolf Laban, who has designed systems of movement based on natural ways of moving. See Rudolf Laban, *Modern Educational Dance* (London: Macdonald & Evans, 1948) and Valerie Preston-Dunlop, *A Handbook for Dance in Education* (London and New York: Longman, 1984).

3. See Psalms 26:12, 18:33, and 20:8.

4. See Psalms 69:2, 14; 73:2, 56:2, 13).

5. Psalm 66:9.

6. *Exegesis* is a process of biblical analysis in which one seeks to understand the original meaning of the literary passage — what it meant for the original audience (including historical and grammatical considerations) — to better understand its meaning for today.

7. For a good study of utilizing the psalms historically in worship see John Eaton, *The Psalms Come Alive: Capturing the Voice and Art of Israel's Songs* (Downers Grove, Ill.: InterVarsity Press, 1984).

8. The text says, "His love endures forever"; however, for the inclusion that God is beyond male and female I have used "God's love endures forever."

Part Three

ENCOUNTERING GOD IN
EMBODIED PRAYER

Chapter 9

THE LISTENING BODY

We ache to taste the wildness of God, where honey and fire meet. We have dressed God in refined clothes like a gentleman, having too much etiquette to be the One who thunders and roars, or comes to Moses in a flame, or to be the One who gives us birth or comforts us as a mother comforts a child. These images woven through the biblical text announce a God so bursting with wild passion, it is hard to comprehend how we could have relegated the Creator to conventions of sterility and predictability. No passion, dancing, spontaneity, spunk, or tenderness are what we are left with, as if God were so polite, politically correct, or controllable that we could actually measure out the passion of God in small drops. If we cannot control the rhythm of creation, the wind, the snow, or the timing of earthquakes, why are we so bold and ridiculous as to think we can dress God in a petite size, shrinking the grandeur from the One who made creation?

Our God dances into history with a fierceness that is

compelling and sometimes repelling at the same time. When we truly come face-to-face with the presence of God, we are stunned to the bone. Is this not why postures of awe accompany hearing and seeing God's presence in the biblical text? Moses hid his face when God was revealed to him in the flame, Miriam dances in the midst of God's miracle of parting the Red Sea, Elijah hides his face in the cleft of the rock on the mountain at Sinai, Paul falls off his horse in the presence of God, and Mary of Bethany wipes the feet of Jesus with her very hair. Coming near to our wild and passionate God calls something very deep in us, something that calls our very bones to respond to this fire of love. Mechtild of Magdeburg, a thirteenth-century Beguine, speaks of this calling with flamelike clarity.[1]

> Wouldst thou know my meaning?
> Lie down in the Fire.
> See and ask the Flowing
> Godhead through thy being;
> Feel the Holy Spirit
> Moving and compelling
> Thee within the Flowing
> Fire and Light of God
>
> *The Flowing Light of the*
> *Godhead 6.29*

The Holy Spirit lives and breathes within us, an ongoing flame of God. Sometimes that flame seems more visible in different seasons in our lives, yet the Spirit is always within us, waiting and yearning to be kindled through our "paying attention." Mechtild invites us to "lie down in the Fire...feel the Holy Spirit." We are constantly beckoned to pay attention to the Spirit moving in our midst by including our bodies in the task of "paying attention." This kind of listening kindles the flame of God within. At times we may spontaneously respond with our bodies, as did Moses, Paul, Mary, and Miriam, but there are also times when we need to intentionally bring our whole selves to prayer.

Our bodies allow us to let loose the wildness of God, to listen and see within and without. Sometimes we think we can control God, the way we try to control our bodies, emotions, or mind, yet we know all too well the grave consequences that attempt has had on people. Men, women, and children are left with rigid religiosity — the fire of God diminishes, and the flames of love dwindle in the need for control. The fire dies if it does not have oxygen or breath; so, too, a part of us dies if we leave our bodies behind. Our breath and bodies can come with us in our journey of prayer, kindling the flame of love burning in our hearts. Bringing our bodies to our spiritual journey can set free the wildness of God within and without. We sometimes think we can control God, like all the rest of the details in our lives, or like our bodies and emotions, feeling sorrow or anger when it is convenient, jumping in and out of a place of contentment or sadness at will. We know how drastic control can be. When things don't work the way we want, we are filled with bitter frustration and become more rigid. We are not open to the surprises that life brings us, for we think that we always

know what is best. We also can extinguish the Spirit of
God dancing in our midst. Our bodies have something
to reveal to us about the fierce beauty of God. This same
fierce beauty initiates a kingdom where lion and lamb
lie down together, where a little child will lead the adults
(Isa 11:6).

The little children may lead us in rediscovering the
passion of God in a whole and redemptive way. Children are unashamed of their bodies and delight even
in their nakedness. So different from most adults, who
are more than happy to cover their bodies. This is not
to say we need to be naked, but let me tell a brief story
that captures the bodily innocence young children so
naturally have. My twin boys, Micah and Caleb, have recently turned two and are filled with lots of wild energy,
certainly more than I now possess. Just watching them
makes me tired; yet at the same time I am invigorated
by their unbounded energy. Still not toilet-trained, they
delight in taking off their diapers and announcing boldly
that they are "naked." The other day they engaged in this
ritual, and I was just about to tell them, "Now, let's get
your diapers on, boys, and get dressed again." My primary concern was having my house baptized with "pee
and poo." Yet they were bathing in the delight of having cumbersome clothes stripped from their little bodies.
Well, I thought, I will just let them delight in their bodies
a bit longer. They jumped, danced, stamped, twirled, and
ran in and out of the room, faces bright with glee, fingers stretching far into the air, all the time shouting —
"Naked, naked . . . I'm naked." Their whole bodies carried so much joy that I had to wonder why I did not enjoy

doing this myself. I do have vivid memories of doing the same thing when I was little, particularly as a three-year-old on the wild New England coast where I was raised. Watching my own children astounds me with the joy all children take in their bodies.

We don't have to take our clothes off and shout "naked" to enjoy the wonder of our bodies, but we certainly can catch joy from the children. They invite us to dance in the midst of our joys, sufferings, aches, dreams, and prayers. They cry out with boldness, "Pay attention to your body, for it is a delight."

There is much talk today about discovering "the wild man" as well as "the wild woman." Recent best-sellers such as *Fire in the Belly* and *Women Who Run With the Wolves* affirm men and women's deep need for coming in touch with something within that has been forgotten. However we phrase it, men and women are crying out to discover the wildness within them, the passionate, the intuitive, the child, the creative, the part that acknowledges both spirit *and* body, the part of them that enlivens and fuels them through life. We are tired of being separated from our bodies, we yearn for connectedness, wholeness, and healing. People from all pockets and professions are acknowledging the negative consequences that dualistic thinking has had on separating the body from the emotions. In the midst of women and men recovering the wildness within walks our wild God. This is the God whose voice strikes with flashes of lightning (Ps 29:3), who comes in a flame, who is wrapped in light as a garment (Ps 104:2), who baptizes us with fire (Lk 3:16), and who carries us on eagles' wings (Ex 19:4).

Wildness connotes the fierce and wondrous, the beautiful and unspoiled, the mysterious and untamed. We are drawn to it in this day and age because we have become too tamed, too polite, yet carrying our anger deep. Cut off from our feelings and bodies, we cry out for something different, forgetting that we have been made in the wild image of God. There is a temptation to control and domesticate everything within us — the movements of deep joy, frustration, rage, tenderness, love, anger, or exaltation. Surely there are a time and place for self-control and discipline, and I am not suggesting we emote all over the place. But I do believe there is so much inside us waiting, and sometimes bursting to come out, locked in our bodies, the good with the bad, both needing to find a tangible voice in our lives. When we become cut off from our bodies, we so easily can become cut off from that part of us that is fire and passion, that gives room for the wild spirit of God.

Anything wild moves. The strokes of the wind, the movements of lovemaking, the cycles of birth, the run of the coyotes, and the dance of the child. We are often awed at things wild, and yet apprehensive. Who can control the wind, the time of birth and death, the northern lights, or dreams in the night? We have sought to control so much that we have forgotten how to listen and live into our dreams, our yearnings and our aches. Our bodies can bring us back to living life fully, to experiencing God in greater depth, to paying attention to the deepest part of us, our natural selves. Often, we are groping for ways to find out who we are. The word *wild* by definition is "the act of living or growing in its original natural state." We need to come back to that part of us that feels like home, or to discover it for the first time — to be free to live into the uniqueness for which we were made. Sometimes we may experience this by owning the quiet side within us. There are times when we need to come to postures of stillness; for even in stillness we move, however subtly. Other times we may need to come to postures of explosion and release. Or we may need to own with passionate boldness the doings of our life. It's all about learning to pay attention to ourselves, our bones, the subtle and bold proclamations living inside our bodies. May we have the courage to pay attention to the fire of God breathing and moving through us, allowing our bodies to bring us through the geography of our inner life. There we may meet our truest selves and our wild God.

Moving from Our Inner Eye

I am advocating that we permit our bodies to be an honest expression of our inner selves, moving from the deepest part of who we are. Some of us may not even know where that place lies, and the process may even feel awkward at first. Giving our bodies their rightful place in our lives is not a one-step process, something we can do once, or accomplish in one workshop, class, or book and *"C'est fini!"* It is a lifetime of ongoing exploration, an adventure into the geography of our body-soulscape.

We need to have places where we have permission to find our feelings, name them, and live in them. Our body movement and body prayer can be one of those places. Many of our experiences, through the sometimes mountainous and even torturous trek in life, are buried within us, even stored in our bodies: deep hurts, losses, disappointments, and traumas waiting to find release in our lives. It is these deepest of feelings that must find voice. They are the inner eye of our lives, and they yearn to be alive. Finding them may be the beginning of healing for many hurts in our lives. But it is not only the feelings of deep pain that must find voice, it is the feelings and qualities of affirmation, strength, or love. Do we have places to be who we truly are? Are we bold and passionate, strong and courageous? Are we steady or erratic, impetuous or deliberate, wild or tamed?

We must come back again to the dance of the child. We often return to the *wounded child* or *playful child* as an adult. I feel we have to come back to the dance of a child or to what some have phrased as *authentic movement*[2] — to move organically and naturally from our deepest selves, where our bodies can be expressive organisms of our feelings, emotions, dreams, fears, hopes, and yearnings, both unconscious and conscious, however wild they may seem at the time. Within all of us we have a lifetime of workable material to communicate through the language of our bodies. The challenge is, as Alma Hawkins, dance educator and dance therapist, says, to "allow feelings to participate in the process of clarifying experience and giving it meaningful form." She goes on to say:

We must not only know how to interact with the external world in a logical and analytical way, we must also know how to get in touch with the inner world and to nurture our intuitive-imaginative response.[3]

Our journey in embodied prayer can bring us in touch with this inner world. The inner world of who we are as well as the ruminations of the Spirit of God within us. But just how do we bridge this gap, from the inner to the outer, so we can move from our authentic selves?

Listening with Our Bodies

Paying attention to our bodies allows us to pay attention to the rumblings within: the delights and joys, the sorrows and losses, the everyday rhythms of our life. Twentieth-century postmodern culture dictates a pace that seldom allows for reflection on the longings of our body-soul. We need to carve time for dwelling in the quiet places, to discover our own inner landscape and the landscape of God. We also must pay attention in the "cracks" of our life to see the "gracelets," the moments of meaning in the mundane.

I experience this more now than I have in any other season of my life, as my husband and I raise our three boys. Lovely, delightful, and energetic as our children may be, our household becomes more and more complicated as we balance our children's daily explorations and activities with family life and work life — the balance of work and play, mundanity and excitement, rest and activity, laundry with poetic inspiration, changing diapers with spirituality. I need those uninterrupted times apart where I can listen to my body and heart, but most of the time I must listen in the cracks. Few of us have the privilege or luxury for hours of uninterrupted time in our day.

Paying attention in the cracks means listening to the full gamut of my body sensations, as well as including my body in the life of prayer and play. They go hand in hand. As we begin to express our feelings, yearnings, thoughts, and prayers through our bodies, we are more comfortable with hearing what our bodies are trying to tell us in everyday life. As we listen to our body sensations, small as they may be, perhaps even our need for rest, a stretch, a walk in the fresh air, we also become more comfortable with using our bodies as an extension of our inner life. The two become one, and we become a little closer to the wholeness that we were designed to live into, with the grace of God.

Listening to the Subtle Sensations

What do I mean by "body sensations"? These could be as simple as a flurry of movement in our chest, a compulsion to fidget, a pit in our stomachs, or a need to be playful. Maybe it is time we went to the seashore and twirled in the sand, or put our hands in the earth and planted some bulbs. Our body sensations awaken us not only to physical needs, but to emotional and spiritual needs as well. Paying attention to my body sensations urges me to ask questions: Why am I prone to biting my nails again or why do I have that occasional pain in my chest? Is something bothering me that I need to attend to? Can I make the time for it? Can I afford not to? Why do I feel so exhilarated when I swing on the swings at the playground? Do I need to make some time for play in my life — am I too caught up in survival?

We all have daily body sensations, but many of us are running too fast to hear them. Even the body's yearning for stillness is a valid posture and one that is the cry of many of us. In the stillness we can hear our authentic selves again. Listening to our bodily cues can be a beginning to the embodied prayer of listening. As we listen, we make the first steps to listening to the bigger ruminations going on within us. We cannot discover the beauty of the wildness within us unless we pay attention to the mundane. It is all about paying attention to everything. Our bodies call us to attention, cry out for attention, and gently invite us to come home to ourselves and to God.

Listening to the Bold Proclamations

The discipline of listening to the subtle sensations within our bodies allows us to feel more comfortable in our bodies. This is crucial as we articulate the deeper things through the language of our body. Many of us may feel self-conscious at first as we begin to release our emotions from our limbs, fingers, and torsos. There are those who may find moving with their bodies as natural as breathing. You may have been doing this behind closed doors in your bedroom since you can remember. Many times students or workshop participants have shared that the only place they move or dance is in their living room, when no one else is present. It is like a secret place they can return to, where they let loose all that is present within them through their bodies. Moving from our authentic self is a journey that begins with losing our self-consciousness, going to a vulnerable place — it is a place that can feel like home. It is being true to who we are, living at our depths, honest to our joys and laments and our places of vulnerability.

There are times when we don't know how to articulate, pray, or cry out from our deepest selves. Other times we are all too aware of our hearts' longings and needs. Some of us may have not been given permission in our lives even to *feel* the emotions that we carry. It is even harder to give ourselves permission to feel particular emotions such as anger, disappointment, or frustration. We may have seen anger released in only negative ways or grown up in a family where feelings were shunned and neglected. Unfortunately many children are not given the resources to attend to their feelings in a positive, supportive way. We are all in some manner "emotionally handicapped." Part of our human dilemma is living with who we are, imperfect and in need of constant transformation.

When we are emotionally blocked, or cognizant of not being in touch with our feelings, it is a good spiritual discipline to express a variety of emotions through our bodily movement. A helpful exercise is to find a simple phrase of movement, one posture, which would communicate different emotions or states of being: anger, frustration, despair, fear, joy, grief, celebration, peace, or trusting. What is it like for you to move with frustration or explosive joy? How does it feel when you take postures of trust or postures of apprehensiveness toward God? Which feels more comfortable? Which do you want to move into? Allow yourself to move from one to another as a sort of bodily prayer. What does it mean for you to express your bodily joy? Is it releasing? Is it a familiar feeling? Is it something you yearn for? These are just aids for us to begin physically expressing our hopes, our emotions, our yearnings, our prayers, through our bodies. The practical exercises at the end of this book will go into this in more detail. Allowing ourselves to enter these emotions can begin to physically move us through our rich inner landscapes. As we physically take on postures of various states of being, we may begin to discern something that needs our attention. It may tell us that we need to deal with an unresolved hurt, or that we need places of celebration in our lives, or that we need to be gentler with ourselves.

Our postures and movement can become active reminders to us of ways of being in the world we may have forgotten or never knew. A particular posture may elicit something deep in us that we need to listen to. Recently I was giving a "body prayer" workshop to a group, and we were sculpting the beatitudes. In this exercise we pray the beatitudes through our entire bodies and enter them afresh. Each group of five or six is given one of the beatitudes and asked to choose a sculptor for their group. The sculptor's responsibility is to mold the group in a posture together that visually expresses the beatitude. Each group is sculpted as a whole, people connected with one another to form a single image. The sculptor is encouraged to stand back and look at the sculpture from a distance to acquire a different perspective. The group I was working with was sculpting "Blessed are those who mourn for they shall be comforted." The sculptor moved us into an expressive posture of mourning and comforting one another. Linked together through different positions, we tangibly comforted one another and could enter into this as a physical prayer. As the sculptor placed my hand gently on another's head, I noticed how healing this posture was. Days and weeks after this exercise I continue to remember the power of that moment when I came away with "listening in my body." I still need to reflect more on postures of compassion and tenderness. It wasn't just my head telling me that I may want to grow in comforting and being comforted, but all my cells cried out with this desire. I will not forget. This is a very simple exercise, one that I have done numerous times, yet it continues to be a place for me to listen to the passions of the heart.

Our feelings, emotions, and bodies, linked together, proclaim that we are alive. Even though we may experience difficult emotions, we are brought in touch with ourselves and God. We begin to taste the flames within and the flames of the Spirit kindling in our midst. This chapter focuses on listening to the entire landscape of our inner life through our bodies. It is the grounding to go on in the journey of embodied prayer in more specific areas: lament, healing, and celebration. We cannot enter any of these with full physicality unless we begin to start hearing, listening, attending, and paying attention to our bodily cues, the bodily wisdom that resides within us.

The biblical text gives us pages and pages of people listening to God and responding with physical postures of response. Not only postures of prayer, which include bowing, kneeling, or lifting hands, but physically responding with their bodies in everyday fashion. These everyday ways can become extraordinary to us because they reveal a God who is beyond all imaginings, wild with love for us. In turn, these postures express a love for God that cannot be contained in verbal response. If the women who anointed Jesus' feet just said a big verbal "thank you," it would hardly have held the same significance. If Jesus just said to the disciples that he would be their servant, it would not stand out as boldly as physically taking their well-worn feet, smelly and tired, and washing them with his own hands. And what did Paul learn in being blinded for three days after his conversion? Did he need a bodily sense taken away from him so he could more aptly listen to the truth?

All of these bodily postures were postures of *risk*. They were postures that relinquished the control of a planned response; they were authentic responses to the Spirit working and moving physically in their midst. These physical postures of response reveal a wild God, one who breaks boundaries, etiquette, and our preconceived ideas of responding. We in turn can allow God to put fire in our bones and sweep the flame of love through our whole bodies. We listen, we respond, we move to the Holy breaking forth in our whole selves. In the hearing we are heard, in the listening we listen, in the moving we are moved. Our journey in embodied prayer is an ongoing dialogue, one that must burn through our bones, lighting our whole body. Jesus taught us that "if our whole body is full of light, and no part of it dark, it will be completely lighted, as when the light of a lamp shines on you" (Lk 11:36). Listening with our whole body, paying attention with our whole body, allows God's ineffable light to illuminate our lives.

Notes

1. Mechtild of Magdeburg quoted in Carol Lee Flinders, *Enduring Grace: Living Portraits of Seven Women Mystics* (San Francisco, Calif.: HarperCollins, 1993), p. 43.

2. The phrase *authentic movement* was first associated with Mary Whitehouse, a pioneer in the field of dance therapy who was greatly influenced by Jung's theory of active imagination. This theory allows the individual to free his/her associations on unconscious and conscious levels. Whitehouse developed the idea of the "active imagination coming through the musculature" and eventually led the client to be in touch with the "Self" (the unconscious that goes beyond the immediate and personal concerns of the ego). See Fran J. Levy, *Dance Movement Therapy: A Healing Art* (Reston, Va.: American Alliance for Health, Physical Education, Recreation, and Dance, 1988), pp. 65–66.

3. Alma Hawkins, *Moving from Within: A New Method for Dance Making* (Pennington, N.J.: a capella books, 1991), p. 29.

Chapter 10

HEALING THE SOUL THROUGH THE BODY

Our bodies and souls ache to be united. They have long been thought of as separate entities. Even in our calling them by different names there is a sense of division; language restricts us. I would prefer us to call ourselves body-spirit or body-soul. We are all one; body affects soul, soul affects body. There have been deep ramifications for leaving the body behind. We know all too profoundly the negative ramifications of abuse on the body and its subsequent effect on our internal lives. Many in our society have painfully gone through the horror of sexual abuse, which is not only an abuse to the body, but a violation of our sexuality — the core of who we are. We are not whole when our sexuality is violated. Sexuality is a sacred part of us, and any violation violates the heart of us as well.

One does not need to experience a trauma to be affected by the split that is so prevalent in our culture: the split between body and soul, body and mind, or body and heart. However it is phrased, the consequence is the same. We are left a fragmented people, unwhole. The gospel message is to bring salvation — bringing wholeness to us. Our bodies need to be included in this process of ongoing transformation and wholeness. Including our bodies in our emotional and physical growth gives us an opportunity to bring healing to this split. This healing may take place on a very deep level, possibly healing some of the trauma of sexual or physical abuse. Or it may just be an opportunity for us to make friends with our bodies.

Through my workshops I have been privileged to walk alongside those who are discovering the opportunity for the body to heal wounded parts of the spirit. This is not something new; dance therapists have seen the power of the body for many years. The power to recover lost memories, the power to bring back the joy of moving, or the power to articulate our emotional life has been fundamental to the field of dance therapy, body-work, or expressive therapy. Dance therapists work under the fundamental premise that the body and mind are inseparable, and thus body movement can reflect inner emotional states; changes in movement behavior can lead to changes in the psyche, promoting health and growth.[1] If physical or emotional damage came through the body, healing can also come through the body. We cannot leave the body behind in the healing or therapeutic process.

The Body As Sacred Place

I continue to marvel when I see my own life and others tangibly changed when given room for the body in the place of emotional and spiritual healing. The body is given a place of respect, becoming a sacred space where God can enter into the work of forming and transforming us. Our own relationship with our bodies can be reconciled; often we are reminded of the relationship we may have had as a child with our physical selves, or perhaps have never had. Sacred places have been traditionally thought of as places "to come apart" and be with the Holy. Thought of as sanctuaries, churches, retreat centers, and even breathtaking places in Creation, many of us meet God in the wilds of beauty: the ocean, woods, prairie skies, or alpine meadows. We come apart from our daily routine to meet the Beloved, to call on the one who we know has touched our lives with the Holy Spirit.

We need to be reminded that our bodies are the temple of the Holy Spirit as Paul so forcefully reminds the Corinthian church (1 Cor 6:19):

Or do you not know your body is a temple of the Holy Spirit within you, which you have from God, and that you are not your own?

We do not want to make the mistake that the Corinthian church had made — emphasizing that the body counts for nothing and therefore it does not matter what one does with it. Paul was addressing sexual immorality in this passage and makes a strong case for honoring the body, one that we need to print on our bones. The Spirit dwells within all of us: body, soul, and mind.

I like to think of each of our bodies as a house with many rooms. Arms, legs, organs, brains, hearts, digestive systems, reproductive systems, emotions, and so forth. We must allow the Spirit to enter every room ... to take company with all of who we are. This may sound abstract. How does one allow the Spirit into the digestive system or into our legs? Yet we so often forget that each part of us is unique and necessary in the full scope of functioning. We work as a whole. Paul also reminds us of this in his metaphor of the body and the church.

> For as in one body we have many members, and not all the members have the same function, so we, who are many, are one body in Christ, and individually we are members one of another. (Rom 12:4–5)

Just as in the body of Christ we are members of one another, so are the different aspects of our bodies members of one another. We have, however, dissociated spirit from body to such an extent that we no longer regard the physical body as a true member in our spiritual journey. In order to allow the body's natural capacity for emotional healing, we need to allow the Spirit to dwell through every part of us.

I would like to invite you to see your body as a sacred space for God, a place where the most sacred of acts can occur — communion with God. In this communing we meet the deepest part of ourselves. Most of us have been wounded in one way or another — through our families, friends, or other circumstances beyond our control. Our brokenness often carries a double dimension that is both emotional and physical. There are life experiences, patterns, or ways of seeing and acting that need deep healing. We will *always* carry a certain amount of woundedness; it is part of being human. We have a "holy wound," one leading us to the place where we cry out for the companion of the Spirit.

Healing comes into our lives in layers. Many of us would like a "quick fix," but the process of healing guides us through a longer journey. We take many things with us on this journey: soul-friends, therapists, solitude, prayer, journaling, support groups, or retreats. God walks, stands, and dances with us in our road to healing. We have been given a wonderful gift in the pilgrimage of healing — our bodies! The body has been underestimated in its capacity to be a healing agent and teacher in our lives. The healing capacity of the physical body is greatly documented. If our skin is severed, it will eventually heal. White blood cells are built into our immune system to be ready healing agents waiting to work with disease and sickness.

Our bodies have another kind of immune system. The challenge is to listen to its signals and ways of speaking to us. We must give our bodies a chance to *participate* in the healing process. The body cannot be left behind as if it were an unwanted child. Our bodies have a voice that will soon let us know when we are ignoring them. What do our headaches, indigestion, fatigue, or aching muscles tell us about our emotional states? They cry out to be united with all of who we are — both in the pain and joy of our lives. As we learn to observe our own body language, we see the connection between our bodily expression and our emotional states of being.

It is not always easy to bring our bodies to the healing or therapeutic process. For some there has been great pain and torment through the body: physical abuse, sexual abuse, eating disorders, alcohol, or chemical addiction — all have profound and disturbing effects on the physical body. Some experiences have caused people to be cut off from their bodies, eventually distorting or extinguishing the capability of experiencing the gamut of emotions.

Common threads of healing emerge when the body is given a voice in emotional and spiritual growth. The first thread is healing the division between the body and inner life. This division, split, dualism — however we phrase it — has caused great damage to us. As said so well by dancer Phil Porter:

> Our culture and our theologies have forced body and spirit into two different boxes, stored not just on opposite ends of a shelf, but in different warehouses in distant cities. Our job is to retrieve those boxes, unpack them and joyfully toss their contents in the air until they fall into one intermingled heap.[2]

The very act of including our bodies, of bringing body and soul together in the life of faith, is an incarnational act of healing, one that begins to mend this long division between body and soul. We are invited to live life more deeply, authentically, and allow God to touch our very bones. In this way we proclaim that we know a Creator who is interested in all of our being, who made us whole, redeems us as whole, and will someday resurrect us whole. In fact this book could be called *Embodied Healing*, for when we bring our bodies to what is most important in our lives, we are always engaged in healing.

Aside from the more general area of healing the split among body, heart, and soul, there are many more specific areas of healing that are reflected in healing this division. I will focus on four of these areas, because these have become dominant in my own life as well as in my own work with people. The first area of healing is in giving our inner child room; I sometimes refer to it as "Dancing Your Inner Child." This area encompasses remembering and owning the joy of being a body, the delight of moving our fingers, walking through the ocean, the sensuousness of the body. The second area is in the area of sexuality, which involves acknowledging our sexuality, and looking at the issues of sexual abuse and gender identity. The third and fourth areas are woven into our sexuality as well, and I refer to these as "Healing the Feminine Soul" and "Healing the Masculine Soul." The masculine and feminine resides in both male and female; after all, we are both, male and female, made in the image of God. In Jungian terms this would be defined as having both *anima* (female) and *animus* (masculine). Both the masculine and the feminine within us may need to be healed, nurtured, or given room to bloom. So, even as a woman, I may need to work on the masculine, or as a male, I may need to own the feminine.

Dancing Your Inner Child

When we begin to dance, we allow play to enter our hearts. Skipping, leaping, twirling, moving our faces and torsos, give us permission to be a child again. Unfortunately our culture doesn't give us many places for permission to be a child. Frowned upon because we may be "acting immaturely," we are resigned to the absence of play in our lives.

At the heart of movement is a playfulness that gives our child room to breathe, to come alive, and, ultimately, to be nurtured. In my classes and workshops I give people the permission to move in ways they did as a child. Skipping, twirling, leaping, jumping, swinging, gliding, and rolling are all basic movements in which children naturally engage. Children skip through the field, roll down the hill, leap in the park, jump in the house, and swing at the playground. My children do all these actions and sometimes all at once on our furniture! Every object is a potential playground to them. When we are invited to do the simple yet exhilarating actions of the child, we give place for that child to be present again in our lives. We invite play into our life.

When the child in us is given physical room to breathe and live, the child is allowed to come out in other areas of our lives. There may be some of us who have not had the opportunity to experience the playful movement of the child. It could have been discouraged, and before long you learn the rules of "proper adulthood." The phrase "A child is to be seen and not heard" is one of the most damaging and stifling things a child could hear. How can a child skip without being heard, or bounce and jump without the accompanying rhythm of the body? One might as well say, "A child is to be still and not to move."

Unfortunately the child learns all too quickly that being still gets more praise than moving. The delight of movement can be stifled out at an early age if it is not encouraged. We can, however, reclaim the world of play, even as adults. Giving our body permission to move again allows this child to heal us, form us, and give us what is rightfully ours — the delight of the body.

Physically appropriating the child within puts what we know in our hearts into our bodies. We so often understand only with the intellect. We need physical activities that allow truth to be known in our bodies as well. Jesus invites us to become as little children. This is a time when movement can bring us back to again experience the delight and awe of moving as whole human beings.

Healing, Sexuality, and Movement

Using our body in the life of human expression puts us in touch with our sexuality. Our sexuality is not something that is just active when we are engaged in sexual activity or when sexual feelings are aroused. Sexuality is central to our personhood, to the intentional design of our Creator. It defines who we are and how we listen to and interpret the world around us. It is a sacred place, a God-given gift.

For many of us our sexuality has been abused, even from an early age. This is not true only for those who have been severely marred through the horror of sexual abuse, but perhaps for the one time when someone violated our personal boundaries. There is no event too small to affect our sexuality. When anything happens that prevents us from fully embracing our own sexuality, something has been marred. Unfortunately we live in a culture that often treats people as sheer sexual objects. Advertisers sell millions of dollars' of products through sexualizing them. The proliferation of child prostitution, rape, and other kinds of sexual violence reveal the deep injustices to the human being. The treatment of people as objects reduces them to a purely physical being with no emotions, mind, or spirit attached. Again, we see dualism at the heart of our views on sexuality.

None of us are exempt from the woundedness in our culture concerning sexuality. From an early age we are bombarded by notions that sexuality is something we can acquire by the right perfume, shaving lotion, or jeans. Even though one can pick up numerous manuals on "how to" do this or that, particularly when it comes to sex, romance, love, partnerships, or marriage, I'm not convinced we've come a long way when it comes to embracing the fullness of who we are as sexual beings.

Sexuality goes far deeper than just having sex. Stemming from deep within us, our sexuality lives in the core of who we are, connecting us to our spirituality. The two go hand in hand. Our spirituality and sexuality are the most sacred parts of who we are. That is why they are so powerful. Powerfully glorious, and powerfully destructive. In my sexuality I relate to the world, to my spouse, to myself as a woman. In my spirituality I relate to God and others as a woman. My gender affects how I will interpret a biblical text, or how I journey in my faith. We bring our precious and our ordinary experiences of being male or female to both our sexuality and our spirituality. Both can call forth from us the need for union: union with our lover and union with God.

The very fact that we have an embodied faith means we have a faith that must embrace sexuality. This incorporates a sense not only of sexual ethics, but of knowing who we are as male or female. We are sexual and sensual creatures, our desires are good and wholesome; it is what we do with them that is sometimes not wholesome.

Sexual woundedness has caused a division between our sexuality and our spirituality. God is the giver of sexuality. Why leave God out of sexuality? We act as if God knew nothing about it. God invented it! To me it is a constant reminder of the femaleness and maleness of God. Are we not made in God's image, male and female, with our sexuality a constant reminder of the completeness of God?

If we have been hurt through sexual abuse, we may not want to awaken our bodies. As a protective measure, we have learned to separate from our bodies. Allowing our bodies to move with God brings the Giver of Sexuality into the therapeutic process of healing and reclaims the union between our souls and bodies. Our bodies can then be transformed from a place of horror to a sacred place, a place where we can apprehend new experiences: experiences of gratefulness and wonder.

An exercise that I do many times in movement workshops is Potter and Clay. Groups divide into two; one is the potter and the other person is the clay. The one who is the potter molds his/her partner, who symbolically is the lump of clay, in some other position than the clay was in the beginning. The person being the clay must remain alert and flexible enough to be molded. They then switch their roles as potter and clay. This exercise is woven into different scopes of learning. Sometimes it is done over a long period of time and used for more direct ways of healing, and other times it is just an exercise done in a small amount of time. In either case most people are struck with how gentle the potter is to them. One time someone said, "It was like the potter was co-creating with me, she almost intuitively knew where I wanted to go and worked with me." This feeling of being able to work with the potter in this way can be a very healing experience. The clay is allowed to be formed in a way that brings out who she is. Her body is physically brought into a new position with such gentleness and care it can be surprising. We need places where our bodies are treated with tenderness. In this simple exercise walls that have been built up for so long begin to come down, and we experience the wholesomeness of our bodies.

It is not uncommon during my workshops for people to begin deeper layers of healing in the area of sexual abuse. Sometimes that occurs by remembering an event that they didn't know before, or it can take the shape of truly enjoying being a bodily person after experiencing a numbness for many years. The act of embodied prayer allows our bodies to have an active voice. Many times we have not been able to have a voice concerning our sexuality. As we begin to intentionally use our bodies in human expression and in the spiritual life, we claim back our voice and dance one more step into our healing.

Healing the Feminine Soul

Women's bodies have not always been thought of as a place of sacredness, or a place of honor. They have been traditionally viewed as inferior to men's bodies, representing the flesh, carnality, passion, and "man's evil desire" for centuries. The feminine body, especially, has been viewed as dragging the soul down, obscuring truth, inner reality, and any notion of the Divine. The Church has a history of associating women with what is carnal and of fleshly character. Tertullian in the second century called women "the devil's gateway." Origen in the third century taught that man is more closely associated with God because woman is fleshly and opposite to anything divine. Augustine in the fourth century denied that women are made in God's image, and Aquinas in the thirteenth century declared that women are "misbegotten males," formed from "some unsuitability of the material."[3] These are only a few quotes, but one could probe the annals of history for numerous references to the evil associated with women's bodies.[4]

The higher virtues of intellect, reason, and truth soon came to be associated with the male. Reason and passion, intellect and body, emotions and truth, were set up to be at constant war with one another. This legacy of male-female dualism, encouraged by dualism in the Classical world, facilitated another dualism equally as damaging.[5] The male-female dichotomy so woven through the threads of culture, theology, philosophy, and liturgy discourages women from seeing their bodies as a sacred place — a place where wisdom resides, a place for communing with the Holy. It also discourages both men and women from seeing their sexuality as something whole and good, something integral to the spiritual life. We are relegated to thinking of sexuality as only a sexual act rather than a wonderful dimension of who we are.

The women's movement has taken great strides in reclaiming our bodies. Resurrected within the art forms of literature, film, painting, poetry, dance, and drama are explorations honoring women's bodies. The long history of negative attitudes toward women's bodies has seeped into our very beings, even on subconscious levels. Many of us have owned these attitudes, if not in our head, at least still in our bodies. Coupled with the reality that our bodies cannot be liked or accepted unless they are a standard size, shape, or tautness, women are caught between accepting what the media suggests is feminine and what is deeply known and felt by them through their own bodies. We have come a long way in recognizing that even our cycles of menstruation are something to be embraced and not looked at with disdain. Yet to have truth reach our entire being — our body-soul — takes not only a transformation of the heart but a transformation in the body. Our bodies need to own a new way of being, a new way of seeing. This way of being has much to do with becoming friends with our bodies, listening to them, regarding them as special, even if they do not come or stay in the size, shape, or tone we may like. Our bodies are a miracle in and of themselves, a reminder that we are beautifully and creatively made. We can use embodied prayer to truly incarnate the miracle of our bodies; it can become an avenue to heal the residue of negative approaches to the body. Here, matter becomes spirit, and spirit becomes matter.

Not only have our bodies been bruised by negative attitudes toward the body, but so has the "feminine soul," that part of us that yearns to respond to life from our gut, from our inner place, and that is also the part that nourishes the creative dimension of life. This is not something only within women, but also in men. Many of us have not honored our intuitive side because we felt that it was not treasured, especially in the executive or academic spheres, the places of "getting ahead." Sometimes we have sacrificed that which is integral to us, and God-designed, to someone else's agenda. We have paid a great price, and the documentation and stories of women discovering "the conscious feminine" continue to burst into being.[6]

Women have built within them rhythms and bodily cycles that cry out for attention. We carry within our being the rhythms of creation — the ebb and flow of life breathing within us. Some women participate in the act of birthmaking, but all women are aware of the capacity for the cycles of birth and death within their bodies. Those who may not be able to conceive, or choose not to, may be even more poignantly aware of the body's capacity for giving life. We have a built-in mechanism that teaches us to honor our bodies, and thus to honor our intuition. We know deep down, in our gut, in our bones, in our blood, that the body is not something to be controlled, but to be cherished and embraced.

As well as speaking generally from other women's lives, I also speak from a deep connection to my own body-soul. Even for me, one who teaches in the area of the body and spirituality, I must constantly come home to listening to my own body. During my pregnancy with twins I learned more profoundly what it meant to listen to my body. In all multiple pregnancies the risk of complications is high, and consequently bed rest is often prescribed as a preventive measure in delivering healthy, full-term babies. My obstetrician advised me to go on bed rest for four hours a day, three months prior to my due date, lying on my side, with my feet up. This posture eliminated the possibilities of reading, writing, etc. I was beckoned and invited to be quiet, to listen to the pulse of my own body, and to the growing babes in my womb. I was finally in a situation where I had to completely give in to my body. This solitary time in an awkward position, which I resisted at first, became the food for transformation. I, a dancer, was asked to stop dancing, levity was given over to gravity, and I was compelled to listen to the more subtle movements of my body. My creative spirit became enlivened and refreshed in the silence. God was creating in my womb-studio, and I was allowed to participate in the Creator's work. Listening to the rumblings in my womb became synonymous with listening to myself and to God. In this time where my body literally took over, I experienced again the importance of creating and acting out of rest and spiritual refreshment rather than my own drive. As my babies were growing in my womb, I was being loved in the womb of God.

As women, we need to have avenues of expression that transcend the traditional language that is so heavily loaded with patriarchal language and masculine metaphors of God. Many women struggle with praying to God as only *Father,* yet the term *Mother* can have equally negative connotations. Part of our humanness is that we often grow up in brokenness — manifesting itself in one form or another in our families — so that even the words *mother* and *father* can have limiting associations for some. There is no one metaphor that is adequate for God. Possibly this is the reason for such a wide spectrum of metaphors for God in the biblical text: rock, judge, eagle, hen, flame, mother, father, etc.

One of the gifts of embodied prayer is that it is a language that transcends the stereotypical traps of verbal language. As one utilizes the body in the language of prayer, one finds that it cuts through many of the preconceived ways of imaging God, speaking of God, and praying to God.

Marjorie Procter-Smith in her excellent work on feminist liturgical worship, *In Her Own Rite,* tells of the need to have "emancipatory language," as opposed to nonsexist language that seeks to avoid gender-specific terms or inclusive language that seeks to balance gender ref-

erences. She defines emancipatory language as seeking
to transform language use and to challenge stereotypical
gender references.[7] She goes on to articulate how emancipatory language assumes God is engaged in women's
struggles for emancipation, even to the point of iden-
tifying with those who struggle. This kind of language
seeks to make women's experience visible and recognizes
the physical realities of women's lives. There is a need to
recover women's memory. She says:

> Because of the church's habitual fear and abhor-
> rence of women's bodies and their functions, our
> language, especially our theological language, has
> either obscured or romanticized women's physi-
> cal reality. Therefore emancipatory language seeks
> ways of speaking which are not limited to identify-
> ing women by our sexual function (such as virgin,
> mother, or wife). It seeks ways of speaking which
> foster respect and love for women's bodies in place
> of fear and hatred.[8]

There is a need for emancipatory language in the
Church which includes the verbal, visual, and physical
dimensions of reality. Embodied prayer can give us a
glimpse of language that can begin to be emancipatory
for women as well as for men. Many of us need new avenues of language to speak to God, and to hear from
God. This is a time for recovering creative language, poetic language — language of the heart and body — not
only to be engaged by a few, but by the entire community of faith. Many times it is only the priest or pastor

who gets to include his or her hands in worship. As communities of faith, we need to find ways that we can more fully participate in together in exploring the use of our bodies as a language of prayer and worship. In a time in history when words are loaded with much baggage, this could be a season for using the language beyond words — our bodies.

Healing the Masculine Soul

It seems presumptuous for me to be writing about the "masculine soul" since I am a woman. However, I believe the masculine and feminine are inside us all. I have also had the privilege to observe many male students discover the joy of releasing their bodies in movement to God and find new ways of being a bodily being. Unfortunately there are usually more women than men who take my courses or workshops. Most of the time one third of the class are men, but that is not always the case. And there is certainly no predicability about the kind of man interested in exploring bodily prayer. There are all shapes, sizes, professions, and personality types, just as there are all kinds of women who come to explore the bodily dimension of faith. There is, however, a stigma in our culture, which looks on dancing for men as "sissy stuff." It happens early, as my first-grade son will tell you; his classmates think dancing is for girls. At this most imaginative age, the possibilities for creatively moving are being written out of their beings.

It is to walk against the flow for men to explore the

bodily dimension of faith in Western culture. Of course, in other cultures it is only the men who dance. For example, in many of the countries in Africa, men readily dance. As said by Pearl Primus, an African dancer, "The African dances his hunger, his joy, his things you have no word for...and in the dance, the African believes that he is in the presence of the Creator."[9] In some cultures it would be strange not to dance, as so well put by Boka di Mpasi Londi: "A festive or sacred occasion in Africa without dancing is like a body without life in which there is no communion with the world."[10] Recently, in the media, we saw images of South African men and women dancing in celebration of Nelson Mandela coming into leadership. To see Nelson Mandela spontaneously moving his limbs in joy was a physical reminder of freedom.

In light of how difficult it is for men in Western culture to dance, I have been very thankful for the men in my classes who have shared their experiences in dancing out their spiritual journey. Many of them have longed to nurture, develop, and give birth to the creative within them. Some have felt locked in a body, trapped by culture's preconceived ideas about how to move. I remember one man in my class saying, "I'm so glad you lead us in doing all those strong movements into the ground, I thought we'd only be doing light movements up in the air." Men and women move differently, but we need each other to stretch our movement vocabulary. If any of us think we have to move in just a certain way, we extinguish the fires of creativity and quench God's Spirit.

Just as women need to reclaim their voices, so do men. It is not surprising that an integral part to some of the men's movement is integrating dance and chanting. Men crave to use their bodies so they can exclaim with all of their being! Men will not give a halfhearted note of cheer when their favorite hockey or football team wins; instead, their arms go out with gusto and raise in the air with a voice of celebration. They are given permission to include their bodies in the ritual of watching sports. There is a need for them to have that same permission to bring their bodies to other parts of expression and growth. Men, as well as women, can discover both "the masculine" and "the feminine" within them by opening up their bodies to the dimension of prayer.

Notes

1. See Levy, p. 1.
2. Cynthia Winton-Henry and Phil Porter, *Body and Soul: Excursions in the Realm of Physicality and Spirituality* (Oakland, Calif.: Wing It! Press, 1993), p. 80.
3. See Jane Aldredge Clanton, *God and Gender* (New York: Crossroad, 1990), p. 41.
4. For a thorough treatment of the history of women's bodies in Christianity, see Margaret R. Miles, *Carnal Knowing: Female Nakedness and Religious Meaning in the Christian West* (New York: Random House, Inc., Vintage Books, 1989).
5. For a more thorough discussion of this see Rosemary Radford Ruether, "Motherearth and the Megamachine: A Theology of Liberation in a Feminine, Somatic and Ecological Perspective" and Elisabeth Schüssler Fiorenza, "Feminist Spirituality, Christian Identity, and Catholic Vision" in *Womanspirit Rising: A Feminist Reader in Religion* (San Francisco, Calif.: HarperCollins, 1979).
6. A few good examples of this can be found Marion Woodman, with Kate Danson, Mary Hamilton, and Rita Greer Allen, *Leaving My Father's House: A Journey to Conscious Feminin-*

ity (Boston, Mass.: Shambhala Publications, 1992) and Mary Catherine Bateson, *Composing a Life* (New York: Penguin-Plume, 1990).

7. Marjorie Procter-Smith, *In Her Own Rite: Constructing Feminist Liturgical Tradition* (Nashville, Tenn.: Abingdon, 1990), p. 63.

8. Procter-Smith, p. 69.

9. Pearl Primus quoted in Davies, p. 8.

10. Quoted in Davies, p. 8.

Chapter 11

LAMENT

Moving Through Grief

୨

Deep calls to deep
in the roar of your waterfalls;
all your waves and breakers
have swept over me.
              (Ps 42:7 NIV)

The motions of grief remind us that grief dwells in our bodies. When we get in touch with our deepest pain, we weep not only with the tears of our heart, but with our whole beings. Our bodies shed water and shake as our lung cavity gasps for air between sobs. We physically mourn. Grief reminds us that words are not enough for our deepest longings. Our deepest longings may not only be for a loved one lost but for many other losses we face in the course of our lives: loss of job, dreams, or expectations, emotional or physical illness, a severed relationship, or even our ache for the presence of God. Our grief is not always articulated clearly

in neat, orderly sentences; the spontaneous sentences of
our body movement may communicate the feelings of
our heart more clearly. The language of clenched fists,
hunched shoulders, sunken bodies, and outstretched
torsos speaks more of the language of grief than verbal
language saying, "I am grieving," or "This is a difficult
time for me."

The language of grief is the language of lament. Lament, which literally means "to show outward expression
of sorrow," has had a place throughout the community
of faith in the biblical text, so much so that it has been
noted that 43 percent of the psalms in the Old Testament are psalms of lament: psalms that cry out in anger,
hopelessness, despair, or grief.[1] We need to find places
for lament in our spiritual journeys, liturgies, and worship services. Only in being attentive to lament can we
honor our grief and pass through it. Otherwise grief can
lodge in our body-soul in destructive ways, eating us to
our very core.

Researchers and behavioral scientists have spent ample time documenting bodily or somatic signs of grief.
The biological aspects of grief can include tightness in
the throat, shortness of breath, sighing, an empty feeling in the abdomen, lack of muscular power, and general
tension.[2] Other biological aspects of grief have also been
recognized, including changes in appetite, blood pres-
sure, cardiovascular function, and even alterations in the
immune system.[3] This is not to mention the emotional
manifestations that accompany grief, such as sadness,
guilt, anxiety, loneliness, anger, and deep yearning for
whom or what we have lost.

Grief is intense, and if scientists document it, poets and artists grip us with the physical and emotional command it has over us. Listen to poet Luci Shaw expressing her grief over her dying husband in bodily metaphors:

> I find it strange how sometimes the reality of cancer recedes, turns shadowy and distant. In the company of friends, we laugh and talk as if all were well, as if our lives were under control. At other times, the horror comes so close it bruises your chin and squeezes the breath out of you.[4]

Death truly removes the breath of life, but the horror of loss changes the rhythm of our own breath. Even our posture can change during the grieving process; sunken shoulders, drooping neck, or caving in of the upper torso. Noted years ago, initially by Darwin in 1872, there are a wide variety of ways that posture, gesture, and facial expression accompany grief and suffering in general.[5] The question that I would like to raise is: If grief is revealed through our bodies, could not our bodies be a healthy form of physical and emotional expression for grief? If changes in posture, gesture, and movement accompany grief, can we include gesture, posture, and movement within our laments and prayers, and ultimately in grief recovery? This seems so apparent to me as a dancer, and one who has used my entire body-spirit to express grief, that I am surprised that this has not been explored more by those in the behavioral sciences and in the field of psychology.

Creating Space for Grief

Grief is unpredictable; we cannot manage it like our time, deciding this is the time to grieve and this isn't. Our first task is to be attentive to the pain, allowing it to take shape in our lives, moving through it, and ultimately allowing grief to transform us. It is a time when our cries can be our prayers and our prayers can be our cries. The cries, groans, and prayers of our hearts can take shape through movement. This may be only a private language between ourselves and God, but there also may be times for expressing lament within the context of community. Let me give a few examples of private and community lament that incorporate movement in the prayers and cries of lament.

Personal Embodied Lament

The first example is my own personal experience with grief. My deepest experience of loss was when both my parents died within a time span of eight months. I am an only child, and even though I was an adult at the time of their death, my mother and father were dearly loved and intimately woven into my life. During the long grieving process, my body became an extension of the flood of feelings that overwhelmed me. Words did not suffice for the pain that continued to sweep over me, but my body could give tangible form to the sorrow buried within my heart and bones. I would often go apart in my basement and dance my grief; the contracted motions of pain, the heavy feet of anger, the reaching arms of loss, and eventually the quiet resting of acceptance. My body faithfully brought me through the passages of grief, as I danced my lament in the presence of God.

These passages or cycles of grief became visible in a cyclical, rather than linear, fashion. The stages of grief originally noted by Elisabeth Kübler-Ross, such as denial, bargaining, anger, depression, and finally acceptance, are not stages that one always goes through in a neat, direct fashion.[6] These are a beginning in the process of grief resolution, but there cannot be one model for resolving all grief issues. As C. S. Lewis chronicles in his own journey through grief, "Grief is like a long valley, a winding valley where any bend may reveal a totally new landscape. Sometimes the surprise is the opposite one; you are presented with exactly the same sort of country you thought you had left behind miles ago."[7] In grief we return again and again to the stages that we went through before — this is the anatomy of loss. The significance of physically dancing my grief was that I gave myself permission to tangibly "be" in these different stages. Grief was given tangible form in dance; this form clarified my experience, which could not be articulated in another medium at the time. In essence the "psychological pus" in my body was extracted and could take shape in a sacred ritual of movement — a personal ritual between myself and God.

My embodied grief gave me the opportunity to dwell in God's presence in brokenness, anger, hurt, and abandonment. I didn't feel I had to rush through these painful feelings and push to some resolution. My body became a sacred place where I could experience God's graciousness as the waterfalls of grief swept over me. I could be broken, and it was okay, I could be angry, and it was okay. My lament was cherished by God as much as my praise in other times of my life. In my lament, I acknowledged that the richness of love was taken from me, special relationships were stripped from my life; these are good things, and they are worth lamenting. Grief reminds us of the treasures we have been given — the capacity for love, joy, friendship, sisterhood, brotherhood, and also the capacity for deep sorrow and loss.

No matter what our grief is, we are left in nakedness, totally unmasked before ourselves, others, and God. It is the place that David found himself in during a time of anguish and unrest and crying, "All my longings lie open before you, O Lord; my sighing is not hidden from you" (Ps 38:9, NIV). David was naked in his lament, coming to God with the sighs of transparency. As we enter into our own nakedness, we allow ourselves to be clothed by God. Here again is the gift of embodying grief; we give God the opportunity to enclose us in tender arms and be rocked in the breast of God. We can truly enter into the psalmist's words: "The Lord is near to the brokenhearted and saves the crushed in spirit" (Ps 34:18).

Community-Embodied Lament

There are also times when we need to recognize the need to lament within our larger communities, particularly within our churches. One might say, "That is what we have funerals for"; however, there is also a far greater need to lament so much of the agony we experience on earth: injustice, war, famine, physical, emotional and sexual abuse, people dying of AIDS, unemployment — the list could go on for pages. Usually we do not recognize our need to lament until we experience personal loss. However, there is a need for us to lament as communities: to carry one another's laments to voice our laments and enable others to voice laments that may never have been articulated. There is a time to come to church and lament the injustices in our world, in our neighborhood, or in our own families.

If we deny ourselves the opportunity to voice our laments as a community, we deny one another the gift of compassion as well. There can be something extraordinarily healing in having a community of faith carrying each other's laments. Several years ago I had the opportunity to be part of a liturgy where we designed "lament" as our theme. We gave opportunity for people to use lament as a way of communicating with God. Our laments were collectively read, sung, prayed through gesture, and danced. We learned and groped together to find the meaning of truly crying out to the living God. For most, this was the first time this group of people were given permission to see lament as an appropriate form of worship. God was able to meet us at our deepest longings.

The Biblical Pattern of Embodied Lament

We need to be granted permission to lament. Many of us have not had permission to lament or grieve, at least not without a limited timetable placed on grieving. Cultural factors are by far the major factor in the sanctioned expression of grief. There is a wide range of permissible ways in which to grieve that vary in each culture. Some cultures have room to express anger or fear; whereas other cultures, such as those in North America, are known to conceal their anger in grief.[8] One of the cultures that has given a place for lament and established a relationship between emotional grief and bodily expression is the ancient Hebrew culture. Lament in the biblical tradition was considered good and wholesome, not just a cathartic response of difficult emotions but a path to walk on so one could encounter God in the midst of pain.

The ancient Hebrew culture was influenced by societies of the ancient Near East where there was ample use of bodily response to emotional grief.[9] Various postures and gestures came to be associated with mourning, just as certain kinds of dance came to be associated with rejoicing. "Beating the breast" came to be synonymously associated with mourning. Pouring dust on the head or body was used in mourning rites of the Israelites.[10] For example, when Job's friends came to console him, they saw him from afar, sores covering his body, and they hardly recognized him. Their immediate response was to raise their voices and weep, tear their robes and throw dust on their heads (Job 2:12).

A posture of sitting on the ground or on a stool was the appropriate position for the mourner.[11] Falling or whirling oneself on the ground was in itself an expression of deep grief.[12] Listen to the psalmist's words of bodily grief:

> Rouse yourself! Why do you sleep, O Lord?
> Awake, do not cast us off forever!
> Why do you hide your face?
> Why do you forget our affliction and oppression?
> For we sink down to the dust;
> our *bodies* cling to the ground.
> Rise up, come to our help.
> Redeem us for the sake of your steadfast love.
>
> (Ps 44:23–36)

The Hebrew word used for bodies, in the above psalm, is literally translated *bellies*. I find this very interesting in light of my own personal movement in lament, as I would continually find myself working on the ground, with deep contractions from the center of my torso: my belly. The ancient Hebrews knew something intuitively about movement that modern dancers would later build into their vocabulary, working on the floor and working from the center of their torsos. It is a primal response when stricken with grief to have the upper torso cave in, with the person perhaps curling into a ball or, as the Hebrews did, clinging to the ground with the belly.

These postures are not necessarily directives to emulate in our expression of grief. It is not that we should all start putting dust on our heads, or cling to the ground with our bellies. What we can gain from this heritage is to recognize the importance of a community giving space for lament and allowing it to take physical form. What a wonderful tradition to build on! Woven already into the Scriptures, particularly in the psalms, is a manual for lament. We can be inspired by the poetry of the people of God crying out in the whispers and cries of their whole bodies. These are so suitable to use as jumping-off points for bodily meditations on lament.

It is also helpful for us to write, sculpt, or draw our laments. Even our sculptures, writings, or drawings may give us seeds that we can interpret to movement. Giving form to our grief is a symbolic act. Symbols may take the shape of texture, colors, movement, words, rhythms, and harmony. Depending on the kind of grief, it is important to search out various artistic media. One woman who was dealing with the loss of her newborn found creating sculptures a healing form. This can be a prayer in and of itself. Listen to this woman's experience:

> I found that after the creation of a few sculptures, I felt relief as each emotion appeared in clay where I could hold it, caress it and form it into a complete statement of what I was feeling. By adding prose, each became more complete.[13]

The important component in all of this is that we find tangible form for our inner grief. There is not one act, symbol, artistic medium, ceremony, or ritual that will resolve all the waves of grief. The nature of grief is lengthy, and it is therefore important that we respect this process.

At one point we may need to dance our grief, another time we may need to write. There may be a time of silence. In attending to our laments, we name them and cry out to the one who can hold our tears. Sometimes all we have to offer God is our tears, and even this can be a prayer. Our cries ultimately become our prayers. Even those laments that cannot be articulated or find form are recognized by God. As Macrina Wiederkehr has said in *A Tree Full of Angels*, "God recognizes the cry of my heart as prayer."[14] The psalmist echoes this as well in saying, "Even before a word is on my tongue, O Lord, you know it completely" (Ps 139:4).

As you consider weaving lament into the cycle of your prayer life, may you be reminded that your lament is cherished by God. I am often reminded of how my own children are struck by sorrow. It may not be anything monumental like a death or social injustice, but if it is important to them, it is therefore important to both my husband and myself. I try to let them know that it is okay to cry and it is okay to be upset. I want to be there to cherish them in their hurt. In fact, I often feel more tender with them at this time, and they, too, are more willing to be snuggled and held for a moment in their mom or dad's arms. God has far more compassion with our laments than I can have with the hurt of my three children. We need to be reminded of God's heart for our laments. Jesus wept. God has compassion on us as a mother and father, a womb-love, ready to embrace the swells of sorrow in our hearts and bodies.

Notes

1. See Bernhard W. Anderson, *Out of the Depths: The Psalms Speak for Us Today* (Philadelphia: Westminster Press, 1970), pp. 169–70.

2. Many have done study in this area. See Erich Lindemann in his pivotal study "Symptomatology and Management of Acute Grief," *American Journal of Psychiatry,* 101:141–48 (1945).

3. See Robin Andrew Haig, *The Anatomy of Grief: Biopsychosocial and Therapeutic Perspectives* (Springfield, Ill.: Charles C. Thomas Publisher, 1990), pp. 26–29.

4. Luci Shaw, *God in the Dark: Through Grief and Beyond* (Grand Rapids, Mich.: Broadmoor Books, 1989), p. 49.

5. For a thorough study of the relationship between posture and grief see Charles Darwin, *Expression of the Emotions in Man and Animals* (Chicago and London: The University of Chicago Press, 1872, 1965).

6. See Elisabeth Kübler-Ross, *On Death and Dying* (New York: Macmillan, 1969).

7. C. S. Lewis, *A Grief Observed* (New York: Bantam, 1961), p. 69.

8. For a thorough study of cultural practices of grief see Paul C. Rosenblatt, Patricia R. Walsh, and Douglas A. Jackson, *Grief and Mourning in Cross-Cultural Perspective* (New Haven, Conn.: HRAF Press, 1976).

9. For a detailed analysis of postures and gestures that were associated with mourning, see Mayer I. Gruber, *Aspects of Nonverbal Communication in the Ancient Near East,* Vol. II (Rome: Biblical Institute Press, 1980).

10. See 2 Samuel 1:2, 15:32; Nehemiah 9:1; Job 2:12; Joshua 7:6; Lamentations 2:10; Ezekiel 27:30; Esther 4:3.

11. See Ezekiel 26:16; Isaiah 47:1; Lamentations 2:10; Jonah 3:6; Job 2:8.

12. See Joshua 7:6; Ezekiel 9:8, 11:13, Job 1:20.

13. Fritsch in Alicia Skinner Cook and Daniel S. Dworkin, *Helping the Bereaved: Therapeutic Interventions for Children, Adoles-*

cents, and Adults (San Francisco, Calif.: HarperCollins, 1992), p. 85.

14. Macrina Wiederkehr, *A Tree Full of Angels* (San Francisco, Calif.: HarperSanFrancisco, 1990), p. 40.

Chapter 12

DANCE AS CELEBRATION

❧

Joy burst through my fingertips, and even my blood had to dance. The heights of emotion have always been difficult for me to contain without a bodily response. My body cannot contain that which rises deep within my bones. It must be given form: an outward incarnation to express the inner reality. I had experienced an enlivening of my faith; the love of Christ became tangible and real. After several years of soul-searching through various forms of religious expressions, I had begun to find deep meaning in the life of Christ. I was being led home, home into the arms of the One who was wooing me for these past four years through college. My cells, blood, and bones wanted to dance. Even though I was an art major, I was yearning to explore movement as an artistic medium. Something new was being born within me, yet it felt very old. It was my body becoming alive, yearning to be included in my journey. Just as my soul had been deeply touched, my body was, too. I recalled the feelings I had when I was a child: the feeling of dancing on the beach or twirling with abandonment in my living room. I knew this experience of God was not just for my head but for all of me. My limbs, torso, and fingers were aching to dance with the presence of God.

The psalmist proclaims, "You turned my wailing into dancing; you removed my sackcloth and clothed me with joy, that my heart may sing to you and not be silent" (Ps 30:11–12). My acknowledgment of God's advent in my life was an experience of being clothed with joy. That joy was a moving joy — one that could not remain in a stilted posture but had to find expression in physical form, moving to the new sounds of love resounding in my body-soul. God's advent is not a onetime coming but a continual coming, a coming that is representative of ebb and flow, darkness and light, presence and absence. There are times of deep presence, recognizing God's coming to us — even in the darkness. And there are times for us to celebrate, and celebration almost always is cause for movement.

My experience so long ago of wanting to dance as God birthed something new in me was very odd at that time. I had never seen such a thing, nor was I exposed to dance in a church, nor did I have any formal training in this manner. However, as I look back at the formative influences in my life concerning the nurture of the "dancer" within me, I find the model of my mother. My mother was an exceptionally creative women: a visual artist and flower arranger, full of life and love for the sensuous in color, texture, shape, and movement. For years, before I was born, she had studied ethnic dance, particularly classical Indian dance. I grew up with her dancing those graceful movements of arms and torso to the expressive rendering of story. Hands, arms, fingers, joined in graceful harmony, became the words for sun, beauty, love, and so forth. Each gesture and motion had a symbolic meaning. Many times when we had company, she would clear out the living room and dance the motions of life filling her body-soul. Because of many circumstances, particularly around the issues of being immigrants, she had far less opportunity than I have had to develop my love for dance. But her attention to dance, for the sake of love, formed something very special inside me. As Isadora Duncan, the famous modern dancer who was part of my mother's generation, said about dance, "It is always in my heart; it blooms at each of my steps. . . . The dance is love, it is only love, it alone, and that is enough."[1] My mother conveyed that love — the love for life, the love for dance, and the gratitude for being a bodily creature — through her dances in the living room. In a mysterious kind of way, it birthed my own pilgrimage of using dance as an expression of the spiritual life.

My personal response to the fullness of what God was initiating in my life would in some ways naturally take expression in my body. That initial response has inspired me for almost two decades, as I seek to bring together dance and celebration. Since then I have been privileged to celebrate God through dance with many others in the community of faith.

As we saw in the Old Testament, *rejoicing*, which literally means "to be full of joy," was synonymous with celebration and dancing. In Hebraic culture dance was associated with joy, but particularly to joy as a *response* to

God's grace. Joy comes as a response to the Holy One coming time and time again into the Israelites' daily lives. God comes giving manna; being fed from the bread of the Holy One is cause enough for joy. It is the deep joy that can't be contained only in the head, reserved for set responses; it's a response of the total being. Joy has a way of filtering through the bones, bringing life and sustaining life even in the dark. Joy is not only like happiness in some special circumstance: It is a way of seeing, a way of being. It is a way of recognizing the fullness of life that God gives to us in the midst of the ordinary as well as the extraordinary. It is recognizing the Holy, the sheer delight of being in the presence of God! Joy is sustained by our acknowledgment, the same acknowledgment that led John the Baptist to leap with joy within Elizabeth's womb. The vowels he spoke that day to recognize the advent of the Messiah were vowels of movement, of leaping and moving in the womb. The dance of joy begins in the womb, and its gestures beckon us time and time again to respond to its birthing. We continue to need the vowels of movement to articulate response.

We do not always have something to celebrate, or feel like rejoicing with our whole bodies. Our circumstances change like the seasons: birth, illness, transformation, change of jobs, grief, the presence or absence of God. However, we can cultivate joy in our lives; joy can come to us as holy listening to the ongoing heartbeat of God's love. To dance is our response to that joy. Well put by a Franciscan monk in the thirteenth century, "Dancing by the believer is symbolic of his [her] active response to God in life."[2] This same joy led people throughout the Scriptures to celebrate with their bodies and leads people today to dance in celebration.

One of the cultures that has retained the use of dance as a form of celebration is the Jewish culture. It is not surprising that the dances of joy in the Old Testament continue through the tradition of Jewish folk dancing. The Jewish people's affirmative response to life continues to be evident today through their vigorous folk dancing. What is so delightful about their heritage is that it gives room for both male and female to participate in joining together in the dance. So often in Western culture, there are few places, particularly for men, to authentically celebrate. Where are the places to celebrate with strength and vigor besides the football game or the nightclub? Should not celebration be at the heart of ritual in the Church? We have much to celebrate through the hope and light of God: Why not enter that celebration with our full bodies?

When I teach my graduate students in my class on "Dance as Embodied Prayer," I take them to the local Jewish Community Center to join in an evening of Jewish dancing. I am always delighted to see a place where men and women have permission to bring their bodies to full celebration. Jewish dancing brings a wonderful combination of levity and gravity, rooted in the ground yet rising out of the earth in quick movements.

Many cultures have a tradition of folk dances, exhibiting a deep joy in moving. Whether it be Russian, Chinese, Armenian, Greek, Indian, or Jewish, the common factor is that dance gives a place for communal celebration. Recently I brought a group of Asian students to the Jewish Community Center to dance for the evening. Watching them enter the dance with the Jewish community in abandonment and joy was beautiful. Asian and Jewish, male and female, young and old, all speaking the language of dance. The capacity for dance to reach beyond traditional barriers of culture, race, gender, and class is part of its universal magic. The language of movement links us to one another as no other language can. We see a picture of humanity responding intuitively to the motion of joy.

Our Yearning to Celebrate

We ache to celebrate. We ache for ritual to again have a meaningful place in our lives. Gertrud Mueller Nelson articulates this well as she says in her writing on ritual:[3]

> What we have lost touch with lies in the poetic aspect of the Church which has always been there for us, which has always been centered in the cycles of our human development and which has nourished us through rite and symbol, through rhythmic repetition. This Church celebrates our cycles and seasons inviting us to see and engage and feel and touch and be aware and grow and be transformed.

The ache for celebration and ritual is apparent in a culture's need to celebrate in one way or another. It is fascinating to me that any reference to religious celebration or ritual is shunned or prohibited in the public-school system (at least where we live), and the only rituals left to celebrate with vigor are trick-or-treating, the Easter bunny, Santa Claus, and other commercialized rituals. Art, music, dance, and drama are relegated to portrayals of leprechauns, bunnies, elves, reindeer, and pumpkins. So much energy goes into these holidays that I begin to think that celebration is intrinsic to being human. If we do not have something meaningful in our life to celebrate, we find avenues that give little meaning in our daily existence. The rituals of parties reflect our need for celebration.

Celebration gives us hope, even if there is no real hope behind it. Many times there is a good reason to celebrate: a birthday, anniversary, graduation, or a ritual signifying an important turning in one's life. I must ask the question, "If there is so much freedom to celebrate such things as Halloween, the commercial aspect of Christmas, and St. Patrick's Day, where are the places to celebrate the joy of God's continual entry into our body-soul? Should that not be an experience to truly celebrate with all our being? Obviously this is one of the purposes of worship: However, we have not always had permission to bring our bodies to worship. This may be one of the reasons we bring it everywhere else and leave our bodies behind at the door of the church.

Again, we can look to the children for inspiration. They spontaneously celebrate by jumping, twirling, hopping, skipping, and dancing as they discover the wonder of their bodies and the wonder of play. When I give adults permission to celebrate with the motions of skipping, hopping, twirling, and swinging, they enter the dance of the child, and something is often unleashed deep within them.

Recently, when I was giving a workshop on body-prayer in a church, people were invited to skip, twirl, and move freely through the sanctuary, as Vivaldi echoed in the background. It is unusual to do this kind of movement within the church, for we are accustomed to approaching the space with much more timidity. There is something very bold about celebrating our faith with our bodies, especially in church. As people were allowed to "rejoice" with their bodies, they allowed God to dance with them in the sanctuary. That sanctuary will never be the same to them, for they have invited God to celebrate with them in their midst in an unforgettable way.

The act of skipping can bring us to something very liberating. We again feel the bodily liberation of soaring through the air. When can we really soar through the air? Why can't adults skip on the sand, in the fields, or even as they walk home? Of course, if you saw your neighbor skipping down the street, you would really wonder! We are so conscious of what others might think, we limit our bodies from responding in fullness to life.

Often as adults we have lost our ability to play, to be playful, and to cultivate the imaginative dimension in us. David in the Old Testament could recall this part of himself. When the ark was brought back in the procession, David literally rotated with all his might, and skipped and leaped. In this beautiful story of David, who is called "the man after God's heart," we see him celebrating God with all of his body. His body had to sing the joy, dance the joy, let the joy move through all the tissues, fibers, and muscles of his body. Surely it was not a prescribed dance, something that one would perform, but a spontaneous dance of jubilation, offered to God from his deepest self. His untamed joy was offered through his body as a prayer of thanksgiving, and he was criticized greatly by his wife. Yet David so aptly remarks that it was *before* the Lord that he danced. That little word *before* reveals so much of David's heart. This was not a performance for an audience or for God, but rather a spontaneous embodied expression of his joy *in the presence* of the Lord.

Where are the places we can dance with joy, thanksgiving, praise, heartfelt and bodily felt worship to God? We may need to pioneer those places. There have already been many pioneers who have gone before us, leading the Church in full celebration. If we look hard enough, we will find the rumblings of physical celebration in some pocket of the Church. It may seem here that we are talking more of worship than prayer. Isn't this book only about prayer? Yes, but there are times when we respond with prayers of thanksgiving, which burst through our bodies to be transformed into praise and worship. For even as we pray, we worship. And even as we worship, we pray. However we call it, we are coming into the presence of God . . . being with God and even dancing with God.

There is a long tradition of celebration at weddings. Many people include dance in this celebration, particularly at the reception. However, I have frequently found myself dancing at friends' or others' weddings as part of the ceremony. In this solemn yet incredibly joyous event couples find they yearn for a full expression of worship, one that echoes the reality of marriage: a spiritual, mental, and physical union.

There are many places where we can begin to integrate our bodies in celebration in the context of faith. Most churches already have a wide spectrum of hymnology, choruses, and music that can be very suitably used to design simple dances of celebration. This could be in the pews, circle-dancing in the foyer, or bringing dancers through the aisles in joyful choreography. We often come together in communities to share meals, or for some other cause. Why not do a simple circle dance as an opening instead of a song? It is something we can all do. It doesn't take gifted coordination, graceful torsos, or certain body sizes. There are many resources to use for integrating circle dancing and other simple joyful responses in worship.[4]

There are truly much grief, sorrow, and injustice in this world. We all will walk through many dark hours, days, months, and even years. When we have those joyous moments of celebration, we must enter them as fully as possible. Our faith gives us far more to celebrate than we can imagine. Surely there are ample problems within the Church both locally and globally, yet God continues to be alive, guiding, walking with, and dancing with us in this journey of life.

Cultivating Postures of Joy

How can we not only bring celebration to our rituals, but also develop a response of joy, a posture of joy, in our spiritual journey today? Cultivating joy may mean different things at different seasons in our journey through life and faith. At times we may have opportunity or desire to respond more physically to joy. The metaphor of dance teaches us about responding to joy. Children embody this as they respond with abandonment and trust — open hands and bodies to receive God in their midst. The posture of dance is not only something lived out in their bodies but revealed in the openness of their hearts.

I often think of my six-year-old son Lucas when his little feet run to give me a hug. He doesn't waddle over as if he was told to clean his room but throws his whole body to running with open arms and bold enthusiasm. He is totally *present* to his posture of love. I can only respond with the same wholehearted affection in my dance of embrace. I want to run into God's arms with the same kind of abandoned posture that my son runs into my arms. The posture of joy. I must again come to God with the same kind of anticipation.

The act of responding with joy involves *risk* and *gravity*. Those words seem to come again and again when I think of both the response of children and the response of dance. Anticipation and abandon. They both have to do with risk. Risking that there is something to anticipate and risking in order to abandon. We have joy because we know the One to whom we are abandoning ourselves. The living God. Even as we continue in knowing and being known by God, we are pushed to risk in our lives. This is where it becomes uncomfortable.

The posture of dance is full of risk. If I jump, I must believe the ground will cushion my body. Yet as I continue to push past my own boundaries, reaching and pulling into gravity, my body takes me beyond where I think I can go. There is always risk involved. When my son runs into my arms, he has to believe that I will enfold him. Even to dance as a child, freeing arms and legs with unfettered joy, takes risks. So does the joy of being alive in God. The risk of being made a fool of, the risk of moving our awkward bodies, the risk of falling.

Gravity is part of dance. The risk to dance is the risk to push past gravity, to risk being confined to the weightedness of our bodies and at times to give in to our weight. Dance not only communicates joy, but the full gamut of a lived life. If we are to anticipate joy, we will also anticipate falling. Gravity will pull us down, but that is okay; it is all part of joy, throwing ourselves into life more completely.

I am pushed and pulled back to trust — that word that is so familiar in our Christian heritage and yet so difficult to incarnate. For trust is made up of all those ingredients: abandon, anticipation, and risk. Trust defies gravity. As does joy. We cannot manufacture joy, but we can come to God differently, learning to receive in a childlike way. We do not come only once; it is a constant coming, pushing and pulling, rising and falling, receiving and responding, mourning and dancing. Joy beckons us to risk — to behold the Holy in all the corners of our lives. Joy becomes holy listening, listening with the anticipation of a child, with the wonder of newborn eyes. And in our joy, in our lament, in our listening, we physically celebrate the constancy of the One who dances alongside of us.

Notes

1. Isadora Duncan in Jean Morrison Brown, ed., *The Vision of Modern Dance* (Princeton, N.J.: Princeton Book Publishers, 1979), p. 10.

2. Quoted in Doug Adams, *Congregational Dance in Christian Worship* (Austin, Tex.: Sharing Company, 1971, rev. 1984), p. 124.

3. Nelson, Gertrud Mueller, *To Dance With God: Family Ritual and Community Celebration* (New York: Paulist Press, 1986), p. 7.

4. Some of these are: Mary Jones, *God's People on the Move: A Manual for Leading Congregations in Dance and Movement.* (NSW, Australia: Christian Dance Fellowship of Australia, 1988) and Martha Ann Kirk, CCVI, and Coleen Fulmer, *Her Wings Unfurled* (Albany, Calif.: The Loretto Spirituality Network, 1990).

EXERCISES IN EMBODIED PRAYER

ço

Beginning to pray with your body may seem like an oner-
ous task to some. For others it may seem as if they've
finally had permission to do what they've longed to do.
We cannot take one class or read one book and then
"know how to" pray with our bodies, just as we cannot
read one book and be able to engage in contemplative
prayer. It is a journey for life, just as any kind of prayer
is. Let your body teach you, for wisdom lies in the body.
Be gentle with yourself, pace yourself, give yourself time.
Time to bring your body home, to make better friends
with your body. You have been bringing your body to
prayer all along, standing, sitting, speaking, singing. We
cannot do anything without being in a body; this is a time
to enlarge what you have already begun, wedding all of
your body and soul in the love of God.

As we practically engage in bodily prayer, do not be
surprised if it will change you. I believe the more of who
we are we bring to God, the more of God we let in.

But there is a certain amount of risk involved. In our risking we will meet the Beloved, but we will also meet our deepest selves. One student of mine who was beginning to explore praying with her body said to me, "I'm afraid of moving because it will change me, but the disappointment would be to move and not be changed, to coast along on a surface level without accessing the real me." She began to taste the risk that was involved as she brought her body to the life of prayer. That risk brought her to knowing a deeper part of who she was and who God was. In her risking she discovered God enfolding her as she went past her own vulnerability, as each part of her body was birthed anew as she prayed with her body.

May you be encouraged to make steps of all sizes and possibly risk an initial time of being uncomfortable. In risking, you may be assured of God's presence with you, of God's tender embracing, acceptance, and delight for you. The Spirit moves, breathes, and dances through you as you journey in prayer.

Bodily prayer is somewhat like swimming or walking. If you walk naturally, you will find that your opposite arms swing as your legs carry you from one place to another. If you really think about it, you'll find it hard to know which arm goes with which leg. You must let your body take you. We usually don't think about whether our right arm is going out first or our left arm is in sync with our legs. We just walk. We let our bodies take us. Let your bodies take you through these exercises. Don't think out what you are going to do first, planning movements in your head. Quietly read the exercise over and trust your inner sensing, your bodily intuition, and know that the Spirit of God dances in you as you pray.

These exercises are designed to do not only once, but perhaps many times. Modify them as you wish to your needs. You may want to spend a week on one, or only ten minutes. Some can be done in groups and are ideal for a retreat setting or informal group prayer. For others you will want to have privacy to extend your body to God in solitude.

Embracing Our Limitations and Wonder

Begin by finding a place where you will be undisturbed. It may be helpful to put on some quiet music, dim the lights, or find a room with natural lighting. What is most important is that you have a place for solitude. For several minutes do a gentle body warm-up starting with your neck and going from side to side. Rotate your shoulders. Warm up your fingers. Clench your fists and release. Shake out your legs. Go through different parts of your body so that you gently begin to loosen the tension throughout your whole torso. If you already do some kind of physical warm-up, like aerobics, walking, etc., this exercise will be good to do following that.

Once you have warmed up your body, lie on the floor, making sure you are comfortable and warm. Try to allow your body to sink into the floor and be aware of the places where there may be tension. Be conscious of your breath, breathing slowly and deeply. This exercise is designed to take you through all the parts of your body and make you become physically and emotionally aware of them. I suggest you systematically bring your attention to each part of your body starting with your head: eyes, ears, mouth, nose, eyelashes, hair, etc., and then going through your neck, spine, chest or breast, arms, fingers, pelvis, womb, genitals, legs, knees, and toes. Basically you will go through your entire torso.

As you recall each part of your body, I want you to reflect on that part, being reminded of the gift it is to you. Begin to thank God for the wonder of being created with such complexity and beauty. Offer each part of your body back to your Creator in thanksgiving. As you do this, you may recall a part of you that has experienced great pain. If you have been sexually abused, for example, great pain or even numbness may reside in your body. This can be a beginning time to ask for continued healing to parts of our bodies. I believe strongly that if abuse has come to the body, healing must also come through the body. Some of you may have areas of physical pain or limitations, such as handicaps or scars from an accident. Even in your limitation you can bring your body to God. May you be gentle with yourself and realize that this exercise can be done in a short time (ten to twenty minutes) or longer periods (one hour) or over consecutive periods of time, depending on your own life circumstance.

We do not often think of all the parts of our body that carry us through the day. It isn't normative for me to thank God at the end of the day for giving me an arch in my foot, or numerous joints in my fingers so I can type on my computer. But as we become aware of the intricacy in which we were formed, shaped, woven, by God, we come to welcome our bodies to the life of prayer.

This exercise is a bodily prayer of thanksgiving for both our limitations and our capabilities. As you begin this bodily prayer, may you be reminded of the words of the medieval mystic Mechtild of Magdeburg.

> As love grows and expands in the soul,
> it rises eagerly to God
> and overflows
> toward the Glory
> which bends toward it.
>
> Then Love melts through the soul
> into the senses,
> so that the body too might share in it,
> for Love
> is drawn
> into all things.[1]

The Flowing Light of the Godhead 6.29

Sinking and Rising with God: Psalm 30

The psalmist uses the metaphors *sink* and *rise* to express our emotional state and relationship to God. Read some of the psalms that include these metaphors (for example, psalms 30, 56, 69, or 73). Give yourself time to read slowly, thoughtfully, and prayerfully. Personalize times in your life when you feel you are sinking and times when God is drawing you to rise. There are many phases one passes through from the depths of sinking to rising to the heights. Most of the time we find ourselves somewhere in the middle, neither sinking nor rising but somewhere in between.

Find a starting position where you can experience how you would sink with your body or try moving through postures on the ground where your weight is dropped and heavy. You may find it helpful to have some quiet meditative music in the background. Try not to think about this in advance, but allow your body, rather than just your mind, to move you through this process. Gradually move to a place where God carries you through various levels, culminating in movement that causes you to rise. You may find your movement is minimal, only shifting heavy, limp arms to a position of strength and openness, or alternatively your whole torso may dramatically move with every muscle of your body, stretching and rising to the heavens. Experience sinking and rising on different levels, in various parts of the room and with different parts of your body, till it becomes your own prayer. Be attentive to the transitions and places of rest, giving yourself permission to be in a place of in-between. Our pauses can be as significant as our movement. God surrounds and embodies us at every stage.

Interpretive Psalm
(For a Group; Ideal in a Retreat Setting)

The poetic structure of the psalms lends itself to breaking them into verses and working on them in a group.[2]

Choose a psalm that your group may want to explore in greater depth. Each person takes one verse and goes aside prayerfully reading through the verse. It is ideal to have a working space that has rooms off to the side where individuals can explore moving in more privacy. Each person is encouraged to interpret the psalm through his/her movement, gestures, postures, dance, etc. Imagine how you would communicate that psalm to someone if you didn't have words. How could that be your bodily prayer to God? I would encourage you to interpret the essence rather than miming each word. This will allow you to reach the heart of the psalm.

Emphasis needs to be placed on the process rather than the product. If your group feels comfortable with sharing, however, I would suggest allowing time for each person to share his/her interpretation of the verse in movement. This will give the group the opportunity to benefit from seeing the psalm embodied in fullness. It also gives the group an opportunity to share and grow together in communal prayer. This exercise needs to be done in an atmosphere of mutual encouragement where each person's creativity is valued and appreciated. An element of risk is involved, but it is in risking that we grow individually and as a community of faith. This exercise can also be done in smaller groups of two or three interpreting a verse together. Remember, it is important to allow those who do not feel comfortable with sharing to refrain.

The Prayer of Opening and Closing

Find a quiet, undisturbed space. You may first want to stretch your body, breathing into your stretch, before you find a comfortable position on the floor. Find a posture that would communicate to you that you feel physically closed, shut away from God, one where you may find it difficult to trust. When you have found that posture, stay in it for a moment. Then I want you to find a posture that would communicate the exact opposite: where you are physically open, open to God. Stay in that for a moment as well. At this point I want you to silently move from the closed posture to the open posture. The timing in which you move is up to you. You may change the timing as you repeat the exercise. You may want to stay closed for a longer time than you are open. Think about making the transition from one to another a bodily prayer in and of itself. Allow the Spirit to bring you from one posture to another and speak to you as you move. Be sensitive to how each posture feels, to which is more familiar, to which you are yearning for more in your life. This is a simple exercise yet can be done over and over again as a way of listening with our hearts and bodies. It is best done initially in silence, so you are not restricted to moving to the rhythms of an outside source but can move to the rhythms of your soul.

Sculpting the Lord's Prayer
(in a Group or by Yourself)

Many of us have repeated the Lord's Prayer since we were little children. It is something we know by heart and mind. I want to give you an opportunity to make it part of your body. In doing this, we again are captured by the power of Jesus' words. This is a prayer that I often teach congregations in simple gestures. It is helpful to move with our bodies, something we know so well by heart, because we can then concentrate more on entering the prayer with our bodies instead of thinking which words come next or dealing with paper in front of us.

Have your group split up into several groups. Give each group one line of the prayer to interpret. Each group will choose a sculptor, and that sculptor is asked to mold the group into one visual image that communicates each sentence of the prayer.

Our Father who art in heaven,
hallowed be your name,
your kingdom come,
your will be done, on earth as it is in heaven.
Give us this day our daily bread.
Forgive us our trespasses,
as we forgive those who trespass against us.
Lead us not into temptation,
but deliver us from evil,
for thine is the kingdom, the power, the glory forever. Amen.

There are several versions of the Lord's Prayer. Choose which one is familiar to your tradition or the one you feel most comfortable with.

After each group has been in a sculpture, you will want to share with each other your sculptured posture. You may want to put them all together in some way so each of you can pray through each other's posture.

The Potter and the Clay

This exercise has been referred to already in the book. It is one I have done hundreds of times with various groups, and I continue to find it very meaningful. As you begin this exercise, may you be reminded of the metaphor of Potter for God. This exercise allows us the opportunity to "live inside" the metaphor of potter and clay.

This exercise must be done in groups of two. You could do this with a friend or in some other kind of group setting. Each person takes a turn being the "potter" and the "clay." The clay's responsibility is to basically be a lump. However, it helps the potter if you are somewhat of a pliable lump and not resistant; otherwise, the potter cannot move you. You may begin your lump by being on the floor, lying down, scrunched over, standing up, anything that feels comfortable for you. You may also want to tell your potter if you have any sensitive areas in your body, so the potter will not get your back out or aggravate a bad knee. The potter's responsibility is to move this lump of clay (you) into another position. It could be as simple as changing the direction of your head and moving your fingers, or it could be as dramatic as changing your level and entire posture. The potter should at times stand back from the clay to see if s/he is satisfied with the new position you are in. I am often reminded of how Michelangelo looked at his sculptures. He felt the sculpture evolved out of the marble, almost as if it was hidden in the marble and it was his task to find it.

Once the potter has you in a new position, you can switch roles, so you each have a chance to be both the potter and the clay. After you have each had your turn, take time to share with each other what it was like for you to do each role, of potter and clay. Which was more comfortable? How did it feel to be moved by someone else? Was it easy for you to move the clay? What does that reveal to you about God molding you in your life? Does it teach you anything about God's care for you? You will find, even if you do this exercise several times, that there will be layers of things to glean from. In fact, I would recommend that you incorporate this several times within a prayer group, Bible study group, or some other kind of support group as a way to receive God's love to you.

A Prayer of Lament

Grief might be something that is fresh in your life now, or you may not be presently dealing with significant loss.

However, we all have experienced grief at some point, small or large, and we continue to grieve for the sorrow we see around us. Where you are in your own personal journey in grief may determine how you want to use these exercises. You may wish to do them over a series of hours, days, or even weeks. Since grief carries many emotions and various stages, I would like you first to write down some of the emotions and stages you have either gone through in the past or are presently experiencing. These could be loneliness, abandonment, failure, betrayal, disappointment, anger, depression, denial, or just being overwhelmed, etc. Write down as many words as you can to describe your experience with grief. I would invite you to then find postures that would describe those feelings. You may want to find one still posture, or to find a few postures. You could also move from one posture to another. If you have experienced several of these stages, move from one to another. Make this your prayer, going through each stage, feeling it through your body, expressing it through posture, gesture, facial expression. Be inspired by the Hebrews and use the ground. How can you express those postures from the ground? Allow this exercise to be a beginning point for your embodied lament. As you feel comfortable with these postures, I want you to image God comforting you, holding you in your postures of lament. You may want to meditate on a few Scripture verses that reveal God's compassion. Some of these may be helpful, but there are numerous ones throughout the Scriptures.

The Lord is full of compassion and mercy.

(Jas 5:11, NIV)

Enter my lament in thy book, store every tear in thy
flask.

(Ps 56:8, New English Bible)

How often have I desired to gather your children together as a hen gathers her brood under her wings,
and you were not willing!

(Jesus in Mt 23:37)

It may also be helpful to express a psalm of lament
in movement. Ones that I have found helpful in working through lament are psalms 5, 6, 38, 40, 42, 51, 69,
88, and 142. Use these as springboards for bodily prayer.
Perhaps you may want to choose a few lines and interpret them in movement. Or you may want to use the
entire psalm.

May your laments be hidden in the wings of God,
named, and cherished. God walks and holds you as you
express your holy grief. As you pray through your tears,
bodies, and souls, may you meet the Beloved.

Community Embodied Lament

The psalms are a wonderful resource to use for both personal and community laments. One of the ways you can
incorporate community laments is either in the whole
congregation or in a small group. A small group can join

in a circle with arms around one another and gently rock or sway from one side to the other, heads hanging. In this way you establish a soothing rhythm, where you support one another. Before you join together, you should each have one verse of the lament psalm you will read. A good way to do this is to copy it on another sheet, and each person gets a small piece of paper with the psalm so s/he can put it at his/her feet. After each verse you can collectively say a refrain from one of the verses of the psalm. At the refrain you can come to a still point that is strong and lift your head up as you say the refrain. On the verses you go back to swaying together as a group. I would suggest you start with Psalm 6, but there are many other psalms to choose from, or perhaps you could write a psalm together. If this is done in a congregation, you can adapt this to doing it in a pew, or in chairs; the people are encouraged to join one larger line across the pews or chairs, so they are joining through the aisles. This symbolically reminds us that we are one body in Christ.

PSALM 6 NIV

Movement is in bold

O Lord, do not rebuke me in your anger
or discipline me in your wrath.
**(1) swaying with arms around one another in a circle,
heads hanging**

Refrain: God has heard my cry for mercy; God accepts my prayer.
(2) coming to still point and looking up with heads

Be merciful to me, Lord, for I am faint;
O Lord, heal me, for my bones are in agony.
Repeat (1) swaying

Refrain: God has heard my cry for mercy; God accepts my prayer.
Repeat (2) coming to still point

Repcat 1 & 2 throughout

My soul is in anguish. How long, O Lord, how long?

Refrain: God has heard my cry for mercy; God accepts my prayer.

Turn, O Lord, and deliver me;
save me because of your unfailing love.

Refrain: God has heard my cry for mercy; God accepts my prayer.

No one remembers you when you are dead.
Who praises you from the grave?

Refrain: God has heard my cry for mercy; God accepts my prayer.

I am worn out from groaning;
all night long I flood my bed with weeping
and drench my couch with tears.

Refrain: God has heard my cry for mercy; God accepts my prayer.

My eyes grow weak with sorrow; they fail because of all
my foes.

Refrain: God has heard my cry for mercy; God accepts my prayer.

Away from me, all you who do evil,
for the Lord has heard my weeping.

Refrain: God has heard my cry for mercy; God accepts my prayer.

The Lord has heard my cry for mercy; the Lord accepts my prayer.

Refrain: God has heard my cry for mercy; God accepts my prayer.

All my enemies will be ashamed and dismayed;
they will turn back in sudden disgrace.

Refrain: God has heard my cry for mercy; God accepts my prayer.

Rocking in the Wings of God

But I have calmed and quieted my soul,
like a weaned child with its mother;
my soul within me is like a weaned child.
                    (Ps 131:2)

How often have I desired to gather your children together as a hen gathers her brood under her wings,
and you were not willing!
                    (Jesus in Mt 23:37)

God will cover you with feathers,
and under God's wings you will find refuge.
                    (Ps 91:4)

Guard me as the apple of the eye.
Hide me in the shadow of your wings.
                    (Ps 17:8)

Find a quiet place where you know you will be alone.
Sit in a place where you can be comfortable, perhaps on

a rug or mat on the floor. Experiment with body positions where you can rock back and forth. Try lying on the floor with your hands held over your knees going to the right and left. Try sitting up with your hands over your knees going forward and backward, your head tucked between your knees. You may want to just lie on your side rocking on your shoulders and back. You can use minimal movement or larger movements. The important element is that you find a rhythm of rocking and be in a comfortable position. You may want even to alter your positions while doing the exercise.

As you have established the movement of rocking, recall some of the Scriptures above. You may want to take just one line and meditate on that, repeating it quietly as you rock, for example, "Under God's wings I take refuge." Image yourself as a child of God, tenderly rocked and hidden in God's large and gentle wings. May this become a lullaby to you, God's embodied loving prayer to you.

This exercise is something you may want to incorporate into your own solitude with God, where you can continue to be nourished by God's tender love. We need to be rocked many times by God's love, nurtured and healed there, to just be present in the wings of God.

Skipping As a Posture of Joy

When was the last time you had permission to skip? Possibly when you were five years old, or maybe with your son or niece. There is something intrinsic to the motion of skipping that is exhilarating, playful, and frees our bodies to soar. And you may wonder how skipping could be a form of prayer. But there is a relationship between play and prayer. Both may take us by surprise. Both may seem like wasting time. One of the verbs in the Old Testament, translated *to skip,* is also translated *to play.* We need postures, gestures, and movements that allow our child to come out, that foster celebration and play. We are told in the Gospel of John that "you will know the truth, and the truth shall make you free" (Jn 8:32, NIV). Let us permit let the truth to run through our blood, sing in our cells, dance in our fingers.

The important element in this exercise will be geography — a geography where our souls can soar through our bodies. An open field, a country road, a park, or the seashore are ideal places to just skip. If you are so fortunate as to live by the ocean, the hard sand at low tide is perfect for skipping. It is hard enough to hold you, but soft enough to cushion you. Concrete is not conducive to letting you bounce around and enjoy freeing your body in skips or leaps.

When you have found a place, or it finds you at some point, just try simply skipping. Skip in big motions, little motions, with your arms in full swing, or maybe down at your side. Do this for at least long enough to let this motion sweep you into freeing your body from the sedentary postures we are all used to. As you engage in this motion, just enjoy the act of skipping. Don't feel you have to think of anything in particular, even some devotional thought; just enter the act of skipping.

At a later time reflect or possibly journal how it was

for you to skip. How did it feel in your body? Was it a familiar feeling? Is it something you want to cultivate more in your life? Does it enable you to let go just a little bit more? Skipping allows us to let go. It is a posture of letting go and releasing the motion through our bodies, the wind through our limbs. You may find it helpful to let this become your prayer of letting go. Letting go your anxieties to God, your pain, your disappointment. Or it may mean letting go your need to have control about something. In your letting go, may the Spirit of God skip through you, and may you praise God in the skip!

Movement As Metaphor

The nature of the spiritual journey is characterized by many ups and downs. It can be helpful for you to think of a movement that would be symbolic of your own spiritual journey right now. Reflect on all the movement terms that could be descriptive of your journey: clinging, walking, sinking, skipping, turning, falling, dancing, crawling, pulling, pushing, releasing, pausing, or leaping. What times in your life are you crawling or sinking? What times in your life are you pushing or pulling? What times are you walking or leaping? You may want to chart for yourself the last month, season, or year; which movement terms best describe some of your life? Try exploring different ways to do these movements, possibly moving from one to another. So, for example, if in my life I feel I had been pushing ahead, I may try to explore all the different ways my body could push against the space, with my hands, arms, legs, or stomach. From doing this, I may feel the need to let go and explore the action of letting go. My movement prayer may be pushing and letting go, moving from these two different actions.

As you enter this exercise, may you embrace a little more of each season. God dances with us in our leaping and our crawling, in our falling and our dancing, in our sinking and our rising.

Notes

1. Mechtild of Magdeburg, *Meditations with Mechtild of Magdeburg*, versions by Sue Woodruff (Santa Fe, N.M.: Bear and Company, 1982), p. 89.

2. It is also helpful to read some background information on the poetical structure and historical background of the psalms. There are many fine books in this area. For a good introduction I would suggest Tremper Longman III, *How to Read the Psalms* (Downers Grove, Ill.: InterVarsity Press, 1988) or Bernhard W. Anderson, *Out of the Depths: The Psalms Speak for Us Today* (Philadelphia: Westminster Press, 1970).

RESOURCES

❧

Adams, Doug. *Congregational Dancing in Christian Worship*. Austin, Tex.: The Sharing Company, 1971, revised 1984.

————. *Dancing Christmas Carols*. Austin, Tex.: The Sharing Company, 1978.

———— and Cappadona-Apostolos, Diane, eds. *Dance as Religious Studies*. Austin, Tex.: The Sharing Company, 1990.

Anderson, Bernhard. *Out of the Depths: The Psalms Speak for Us Today*. Philadelphia: Westminster Press, 1974.

Backman, Eugene Louis. *Religious Dances in the Christian Church and in Popular Medicine*. Translated by E. Classen. London: Allen & Unwin, 1952, reprinted, 1977.

Blogg, Martin H. *Time to Dance: 12 Practical Dances for the Non-Dance Specialist in Education, Church, and Community*. London: Collins Liturgical Publications, 1984.

Blom, Lynne Anne, and L. Tarin Chaplin. *The Intimate Act of Choreography*. Pittsburgh: University of Pittsburgh Press, 1982.

Bottomley, Frank. *Attitudes to the Body in Western Christendom*. London: Lepus Books, 1979.

Brand, Paul, and Philip Yancey. *Fearfully and Wonderfully Made*. Grand Rapids, Mich.: Zondervan, 1987.

Bynum, Caroline Walker. *Jesus and Mother: Studies in Spirituality of the High Middle Ages*. Los Angeles, Calif.: University of California Press, 1982.

Collins, Donald E. *Like Trees That Grow Beside a Stream: Praying Through the Psalms.* Nashville, Tenn.: Upper Room Books, 1991.

Cooper, John W. *Body, Soul, & Everlasting: Biblical Anthropology and the Monism-Dualism Debate.* Grand Rapids, Mich.: William B. Eerdmans Publishing Company, 1989.

Daniels, Marilyn. *The Dance in Christianity: A History of Religious Dance Through the Ages.* Mahwah, N.J.: Paulist Press, 1981.

Davies, John Gordon. *Liturgical Dance: An Historical and Practical Handbook.* London: SCM Press, 1984.

Davis, Charles. *Body As Spirit: The Nature of Religious Feeling.* New York: Seabury, 1976.

Deitering, Carolyn. *The Liturgy As Dance and the Liturgical Dancer.* New York: Crossroads Publishing Company, 1984.

———. *Actions, Gestures, and Bodily Attitudes.* San Jose, Calif.: Resource Publications, 1980.

DeSola, Carla. *Learning Through Dance.* New York: Paulist Press, 1974.

———. *The Spirit Moves: A Handbook of Dance and Prayer.* Washington, D.C.: The Liturgical Conference, 1977, reprinted 1986.

Eaton, John. *The Psalms Come Alive: Capturing the Voice and Art of Israel's Songs.* Downers Grove, Ill.: InterVarsity Press, 1984.

Feher, Michel, Ramona Naddaff, and Nadia Tazi, eds. *Fragments for a History of the Human Body,* Parts 1, 2, 3. New York: Urzone Inc., 1989.

Fenton, John, ed. *Theology and Body.* Philadelphia: Westminster Press, 1974.

Fischer, Kathleen. *Women at the Well: Feminist Perspectives on Spiritual Direction.* New York: Paulist Press, 1988.

Fisher, Constance. *Dancing the Old Testament: Christian Celebrations of Israelite Heritage for Worship and Education.* Austin, Tex.: The Sharing Company, 1980.

———. *Dancing with Early Christians,* ed. by Doug Adams. Austin, Tex.: The Sharing Company, 1983.

Gagne, Ronald, M.S., Thomas Kane, C.S.P., and Robert Ver-Eecke, S.J. *Introducing Dance in Christian Worship*. Washington, D.C.: Pastoral Press, 1984.

Hawkins, Alma M. *Moving from Within: A New Method for Dance Making*. Pennington, N.J.: a capella books, 1991.

Humphrey, Doris. *The Art of Making Dances*. New York: Grove Press, 1959.

Jones, Mary. *God's People on the Move: A Manual for Leading Congregations in Dance and Movement*. NSW, Australia: Christian Dance Fellowship of Australia, 1988.

Kirk, Martha Ann, CCVI. *Celebrations of Biblical Women's Stories: Tears, Milk and Honey*. Kansas City, Mo.: Sheed & Ward, 1987.

———— and Coleen Fulmer. *Her Wings Unfurled*. Albany, Calif.: The Loretto Spirituality Network, 1990.

Koch, Carl, and Joyce Heil. *Created in God's Image: Meditating On Our Body*. Winona, Minn.: Saint Mary's Press, 1991.

L'Engle, Madeleine. *Walking on Water: Reflections on Art and Faith*. Wheaton, Ill.: Harold Shaw, 1980.

Mealy, Norman, and Judith Rock. *Performer As Priest and Prophet: Restoring the Intuitive in Worship Through Music and Dance*. Austin, Tex.: The Sharing Company, 1988.

Mettler, Barbara. *Materials of Dance As a Creative Art Activity*. Tucson, Ariz.: Mettler Studios, 1960.

Miles, Margaret. *Fullness of Life: Historical Foundations for a New Asceticism*. Philadelphia: Westminster Press, 1981.

————. *Image as Insight: Visual Understanding in Western Christianity and Secular Culture*. Boston, Mass.: Beacon Press, 1985.

————. *Carnal Knowing: Female Nakedness and Religious Meaning in the Christian West*. New York: Vintage Books, 1989.

Miller, James L. *Measures of Wisdom: The Cosmic Dance in Classical and Christian Antiquity*. Toronto, Ontario: University of Toronto Press, 1986.

Nachmanovitch, Stephen. *Free Play: The Power of Improvisation in Life and the Arts*. New York: Tarcher/Perigee Books (Putnam), 1990.

National Conference on Catholic Bishops. *Environment and Art in Catholic Worship.* Washington, D.C.: U.S. Catholic Conference, 1978.

Nelson, Mueller Gertrud. *To Dance With God: Family Ritual and Community Celebration.* New York: Paulist Press, 1986.

Nouwen, Henri J. M. *Behold the Beauty of the Lord: Praying with Icons.* Notre Dame, Ind.: Ave Maria Press, 1987.

O'Connor, Elizabeth. *Eighth Day of Creation: Discovering Your Gifts and Using Them.* Waco, Tex.: Word Books, 1971.

Oesterley, William, O. E. *The Sacred Dance in Comparative Folklore.* Cambridge, Eng.: Cambridge University Press, 1923. Reprint, New York: Dance Horizons, 1960.

Ortegal, Adelaide, S.P. *A Dancing People.* West Lafayette, Ind.: Center for Contemporary Celebration, 1976.

Peterson, Eugene. *Answering God: The Psalms As Tools for Prayer.* San Francisco, Calif.: Harper & Row, 1989.

Procter-Smith, Marjorie. *In Her Own Rite: Constructing Feminist Liturgical Tradition.* Nashville, Tenn.: Abingdon Press, 1990.

Roth, Nancy. *The Breath of God: An Approach to Prayer.* Cambridge, Mass.: Cowley, 1990.

Ryken, Leland, ed. *The Christian Imagination: Essays on Literature and the Arts.* Grand Rapids, Mich.: Baker, 1981.

Sayers, Dorothy. *The Mind of the Maker.* San Francisco: Harper & Row, 1987.

Schreck, Nancy, OSF, and Maureen Leach, OSF. *Psalms Anew: In Inclusive Language.* Winona, Minn.: Saint Mary's Press, 1986.

Seerveld, Calvin. *Rainbows for the Fallen World: Aesthetic Life and Artistic Task.* Toronto, Ontario: Toronto Tuppence Press, 1980.

Taylor, Margaret Fisk. *Dramatic Dance with Children in Worship and Education.* Austin, Tex.: The Sharing Company, 1977.

———. *Hymns in Action for Everyone: People 9 to 90 Dancing Together.* Austin, Tex.: The Sharing Company, 1985.

———. *A Time to Dance: Symbolic Movement in Worship.* Austin, Tex.: The Sharing Company, 1980 (rev. ed.).

Van Der Leeuw, Gerardus. *Sacred and Profane Beauty: The Holy in Art.* New York: Holt, Rinehart and Winston, 1963.

Willard, Dallas. *The Spirit of the Disciplines.* (Chapter 6: "Spiritual Life: The Body's Fulfillment"). San Francisco, Calif.: Harper & Row, 1988.

Winton-Henry, Cynthia, and Phil Porter. *Body & Soul: Excursions in the Realm of Physicality and Spirituality.* Oakland, Calif.: Wing It! Press, 1993.

Winter, Miriam Therese. *Women Prayer Women Song.* New York: Meyer-Stone/Crossroad, 1991.

Wiederkehr, Macrina. *A Tree Full of Angels: Seeing the Holy in the Ordinary.* San Francisco, Calif.: HarperCollins, 1988.

Wolterstorff, Nicholas. *Art in Action.* Grand Rapids, Mich.: Eerdmans, 1980.

Wuellner, Flora Slosson. *Prayer and Our Bodies.* Nashville, Tenn.: Upper Room, 1987.

About the Author

Celeste Snowber Schroeder is a liturgical dance artist, writer, and educator whose work focuses on spirituality and the body. A pioneer in the subject of Christianity and the arts with a specialization in movement/dance, she has choreographed and performed pieces in schools, Christian universities, seminaries, churches, conferences, and theaters in the United States and Canada. A longtime student and teacher of dance, Schroeder holds a B.A. in art history from Southeastern Massachusetts University and an M.A. in theological studies from Gordon-Conwell Theological Seminary. She frequently leads workshops for various churches and conferences in the areas of embodied prayer, dance, and spirituality and the arts. She presently teaches in the Faculty of Interdisciplinary Studies and Spiritual Theology at Regent College in Vancouver and in the Fine Arts Department at Trinity Western University in Langley, British Columbia. Schroeder has published articles in *Modern Liturgy, Sacred Dance Guild Journal, Faith Today,* and various other journals. She resides with her husband and three children in Port Moody, British Columbia.